Power of two letters - BABA

Baba Chitra Suresh

First Published by

An Imprint of BlueRose Publishers

ISBN: 978-93-93388-74-2

Price: INR 180

BLUEROSE PUBLISHERS
www.bluerosepublishers.com
info@bluerosepublishers.com
+91 8882 898 898

Om Ganeshaya Namaha

DEDICATED TO

My Family God
Tirupati Lord Sri Venkateshwara

&

My Sadguru Sri Sai Baba of Shirdi

IN LOVING MEMORY OF

My late parents
Smt. K. Janaki and Shri P. Krishnaswami

&

My late husband Shri C.N. Suresh

ACKNOWLEDGEMENT

I would like to express my gratitude to each and every devotee who has shared their experience.

My special thanks to Shri Arun B Ghodke for inviting me to participate in the Palki procession of Baba and honouring me to carry Baba's Palki during the procession which will be cherished by me for a lifetime.

My heartfelt thanks to Shri Vijayakumar and Mrs. Rema Vijayakumar, Trustees of Sri Vengusapriya Saibaba Anandhashrama Trust, Theethipalayam, Coimbatore.

I express my gratitude to the Trustees and Management of Sri Naga Sai Temple, Coimbatore.

My special thanks to Shri Sudhir Ranjan who informed me about the Sai Sammelan where a book launching event is also planned.

I thank the organisers of Sai Sammelan for having agreed to launch the book during the prestigious Sai Sammelan event.

My thanks to Shri Puneet Malik, Shri Vijay Mehta and Shri Uday Bakshi for their constant support.

I would like to thank Mrs. Rani Ravi and Mrs. Rajeswari who gave me ideas from time to time, stood by me throughout the writing of this book and instilled confidence in me and encouraged me when I was struggling to proceed while writing the book.

My prostrations to my late parents who provided good education to me to become worthy of writing a book.

My gratitude to my late husband Shri C.N. Suresh, whose principles and ideals I have imbibed.

Thanks to my siblings and all other members of my family for their ideas, support and guidance.

My special thanks to my son Nikhil Suresh who motivated me to write the book and ensured that I completed it on time.

Thanks to Blue Rose Publishers and their entire team who worked hard to ensure a good output and timely publishing of the book.

Prologue

Believing in the power of Baba in our lives will get us through anything. The very moment I became a devotee of Baba, my life started changing for the better. Today, I am convinced that devotion to Baba can do wonders and can even elevate a person to unimaginable heights.

There comes a time in the lives of everyone, when one becomes lonely, stressed out, oppressed and depressed. The help and support of family, friends and well wishers also become ineffective or sometimes counterproductive and the things may become out of control. During such moments, sometimes one feels lost and some may even end up taking some undesirable extreme steps.

Once when I was at such a crossroads in my life, I got a copy of Sri Sai Satcharitra. I started reading the book and found it interesting and completed the book within a few days. Read it again and again. I visited Shirdi within a few days of finishing Sri Sai Satcharitra. Then onwards I am under Sai Baba's protective umbrella. Sri Sai Satcharitra became my friend, guide and way of life. My life started improving; problems started dissolving; financially became stable; and I started regaining my self-esteem. I could see visible changes in my life and myself. I witnessed amazing miracles in my life. I frequented Sai Baba temple where I could offload my unnecessary excess baggage like worries, tension, etc. and find solace and peace of mind. Having tasted the nectar of Sri Sai Satcharitra, I wish the same to others who are today in similar conditions as I was once.

Thus, germinated the idea of writing this book **"The power of two letters - BABA"** on Sai Baba's miracles.

A quote from Sri Sai Satcharitra Chapter XII:

"There are many persons whose desire for Baba's darshan was not satisfied. If these persons, believing in Him, listen to His Leelas, their quest for darshan will be, to a great extent, satisfied by His Leelas."

Bow to Shri Sai
Peace be to all

11 Assurances of Baba

- Whosoever puts their feet on Shirdi soil, their sufferings will come to an end.
- The wretched and miserable will rise to joy and happiness as soon as they climb the steps of the mosque.
- I shall be ever active and vigorous even after leaving this earthly body.
- My tomb shall bless and speak to the needs of my devotees.
- I shall be active and vigorous even from my tomb.
- My mortal remains will speak from my tomb.
- I am ever living to help and guide all who come to me, who surrender to me and who seek refuge in me.
- If you look to me, I look to you.
- If you cast your burden on me, I shall surely bear it.
- If you seek my advice and help, it shall be given to you at once.
- There shall be no want in the house of my devotee.

CONTENTS

CHAPTER 1	BABA VISITING DEVOTEES' PREMISES	1
CHAPTER 2	FULFILLING THE WISHES OF THE DEVOTEES	7
CHAPTER 3	BLESSED DURING THE FIRST VISIT TO SHIRD	13
CHAPTER 4	VARIOUS DISEASES CURED	23
CHAPTER 5	VARIOUS DISEASES CURED - CONTINUED	29
CHAPTER 6	VARIOUS DISEASES CURED - CONTINUED	34
CHAPTER 7	TIMELY ASSISTANCE	41
CHAPTER 8	VOWS FULFILLED	50
CHAPTER 9	EXAMINATIONS CLEARED	56
CHAPTER 10	BLESSED WITH A CHILD	59
CHAPTER 11	IMPROVED ECONOMIC CONDITIONS / LIVING CONDITIONS	66
CHAPTER 12	DREAM COME TRUE	74
CHAPTER 13	BUSINESS / JOB RELATED MATTERS	80
CHAPTER 14	UDI MIRACLES	88
CHAPTER 15	MAJESTIC MIRACLES	97
CHAPTER 16	LEGAL / PROPERTY RELATED	107

	MATTERS	
CHAPTER 17	TIMELY RESCUE	110
CHAPTER 18	WEDDING DAY BLESSINGS	119
CHAPTER 19	LOST AND FOUND	123
CHAPTER 20	PROTECTIVE UMBRELLA OF BABA	128
CHAPTER 21	GRACED BY DARSHAN OF BABA	132
CHAPTER 22	FOREWARNED	138
CHAPTER 23	TEMPLE MIRACLES	142
	EPILOGUE	149
	ARATHI	151
	ARATHI MEANING	152

CHAPTER - 1

BABA VISITING DEVOTEES' PREMISES

Jayanti graced by Baba

Jayanti Ganeshan from Walajapet, Tamil Nadu, had Baba's idol in her shrine and in the hall. However, she didn't have one in her study where she had the picture of other Saints and deities. One Tuesday, she prayed to Baba that He should come to her and that she will not go and buy herself.

To her surprise the same week on Thursday while she was in the office she received three gifts. They contained Saibaba idols. It was also categorically mentioned that the three gifts were meant for Jayanti and two other colleagues in the same company. This was sent by one of her former colleagues. When she called her former colleague, he said that he completed his seven weeks of Sai Baba vrat and distributed seven idols to his colleagues as per his wish. When she asked him how he knew that she is a Sai devotee and why he chose to give the idol to her when there are around 600 employees in that company, her colleague replied that Sai Baba told, "give one idol to Jayanti". Hearing this and seeing the unconditional love of Baba to His devotees, Jayanti says she was dumb founded and her body was swept by horripilation.

Sipra's wish fulfilled

On July 20, 2021, Sipra Banerjee of Bhubaneswar chanted Baba's name before going to bed. She also told Baba, "I am chanting your name daily but can't visit you as I don't know where your temple is. I want to see you, can I see you?" Next morning she woke up early and after chanting Baba's name repeated her wish to Baba to see Him at least once. After that she submerged herself in daily chores.

Same day, at about 9 a.m. a big truck decorated with flowers came near her gate. This truck comes quite often with idols / pictures of different gods / goddesses. Therefore, she took Rs 10 as offering and went near her gate. But to her surprise, she saw a beautiful idol of Baba in the truck. Tears started rolling down her eyes when she realised that Baba himself came to visit her on her request. One of the persons in the truck asked Sipra if she believes in Baba. She replied that not a single day goes without chanting His name. To this he replied, "that's why Baba has come to visit you". He also gave her prasad and flowers.

The best thing about this incident was that Sipra is a resident of that area for the past around 15 years. Idols of various Gods /Goddesses had been coming often but this is the first time that Baba came near her house. It is also worth mentioning here that the Sai sewak in the truck did not knock at any other house and nobody came outside other than Sipra.

"Baba always runs to His devotees who remember Him with love and affection", says Sipra with a smile on her face and her eyes thanking Baba for blessing her abundantly with His darshan.

Baba having Dal Baath as Bhiksha

Vani Prakash from Hassan narrates her experience that happened three years back. One morning as she was preparing dal baath, a desire arose in her mind to feed someone needy with hot and fresh dal baath as sometimes people give only cold or stale food as bhiksha to many needy persons. She reverentially prayed to Baba to send someone to whom she can offer fresh dal baath. She continued to pray for about half an hour and came out and started making Rangoli while praying all the time to Baba to send someone to accept her food.

Suddenly she heard someone calling "Amma" and when she turned back she saw one person looking exactly like Baba was standing there. She was speechless and couldn't move. After 2-3 minutes she ran inside and packed some dal baath and gave it to him. He took the food, blessed her and went away. Vani says, Baba heard her prayer and fulfilled her desire.

Story of Rajiv Bagga

Rajiv Bagga of New Delhi says, it is strange that his whole family is a devotee of Satya Sai Baba while he follows Shirdi Sai Baba. Once he was fascinated by the statue of Sai Baba in one of the temples. The same night he had a vision of a red coloured circle from which he could see rays were moving from Satya Sai Baba to Shirdi Sai Baba and vice versa with a link between the two. Suddenly he woke up and was perspiring profusely. Once again he had a similar vision more forcefully.

After this incident he says, "I became an ardent devotee of Saibaba and I reverentially bow to both the spiritual leaders". Dinesh says this incident is still fresh in his mind and he construes this as a miracle of Sai Baba to make him walk the spiritual path.

Once while strolling through the shops outside the Baba temple, he was drawn towards one of the beautiful portraits of Baba. He says his words can't explain the magnetic power the portrait had. He wanted to purchase the portrait but couldn't afford it as it was priced at Rs. 15 which was a huge money during those days.

Later on, when he returned home he saw the same portrait at his residence. He came to know through his mother that their local grocer had given this while delivering grocery items.

Rajiv had no words to thank Baba for this kind gesture and he kept that portrait in his shrine and started worshipping regularly.

Shower of Baba's photo

Radhakrishnan of Delhi and his family had been involved in annadanam activities at a local Ganesh temple every Sunday since 2005. Around 400 under privileged children and needy persons had been fed in this Annadanam drive. Radhakrishnan and his family are staunch devotees of Shirdi Sai Baba and a few other Mahants/Gurus. Apart from the annadan service, he and his family members had been regularly involving themselves in various other noble services by extending support to the poor and needy persons.

One day while Radhakrishnan was performing his sewa by distributing plates to the children before meals suddenly from the bottom of one plate, lots of Baba photos started falling down like a pack of cards. No one knew how and where the photos came from. To him this incident was not only a miracle of Baba but he construes this as Baba's merciful blessings on him as this incident happened only with him and not with any other sewak of the temple. He distributed the photos among all the temple authorities.

Baba appearing in the dream of Sripriya

Sripriya of Chennai had a dream. One day she was returning home with Baba's idol. As she entered home she saw her mother (who is no more) cutting vegetables. At that time, she felt someone was behind her and when she turned she saw Baba standing there and saying, "you think you have called me to your house. No, I came on my own". At this moment she woke up and realised that this was a dream. However, she was very pleased with the dream and felt blessed by Baba.

Bow to Shri Sai
Peace be to all

CHAPTER 2

FULFILLING THE WISHES OF THE DEVOTEES

Suparna gets a new dress

Suparna of Orissa says that she had been a staunch devotee of Baba since childhood. Her parents were working and therefore she was living in a hostel. She used to meet her parents 2-3 times a year. She says, "I suffered a lot during the hostel days, but my Sai was always there by my side, to comfort me".

Once there was a function in the college and all her friends had new dresses to wear. Since she had no money, she couldn't buy one. Then she cried a lot at night before going to sleep and asked Baba, "don't you feel bad that I don't have a new dress while all my friends have. I want You to give me a new dress tomorrow for my college function".

Next morning when she was rehearsing for the college event, the gatekeeper told her that she had a visitor. She thought her father would have come as all the parents were invited for the event. But she saw a friend of her father. He gave her a gift for the festive season. He asked her if she liked the gift. She opened the packet and saw the beautiful party dress. But since she prefers simple and inexpensive outfits she asked him if she can exchange it and he agreed. Then with the permission of hostel authorities she went out and got two dresses with the same money. She says Sai fulfilled her wish.

Baba gives consecrated coin to Anuradha

Anuradha, an ardent devotee of Baba says, "whenever I read chapter 29 of Sai Satcharitra and Dr. Captain Hate's experience, I used to pray to Baba to bless me with a coin consecrated by Him."

Anuradha says, "on January 3, 2019, I went to Shirdi with my brother and his office colleagues. Next morning I went to the Samadhi Mandir. Usually I go from the right side so that I can spend more time inside the Mandir with Baba. That particular day I was forced to the left line. I came near Baba's padham (feet) and touched and prayed. Suddenly the priest took a bunch of roses from near Baba's feet and gave them to me. I was extremely happy as I thought that Baba had blessed me with roses. Just as I was stepping outside the door of the Samadhi Mandir a one rupee coin was rolling down from the bunch of flowers. I bent down and took it. When I saw the 1 rupee coin with dry flowers stuck on one side, I just wanted to run and hug my Baba and kiss Him. What more can I ask for? I was standing with uncontrollable tears rolling down my eyes while constantly uttering "Love you Baba, love you Baba".

Thoughts translated into action by Baba

Anuradha from Chennai says, when she went to Shirdi in 2006, a thought arose in my mind, how nice it would be if she could walk barefoot in Shirdi where Baba had walked and the soil is so holy and blessed. However, she dismissed the idea thinking that people would make fun of her if she walked without sandals.

After reaching Kopergaon station they walked only a few steps and her sandal broke. She had to leave her sandals and proceed further. A voice in her said, "you wanted and look here it's happening'. Since they went to Shirdi on a very short trip, they had no time to purchase a new pair of sandals. Therefore, she went all along bare foot and had Baba's darshan. She could buy a new pair of sandals near the railway station before leaving Shirdi.

The above story is a true manifestation of the fact that Baba would fulfill the humble and pure hearted wishes of His devotees in His own peculiar ways.

Sai blesses His devotee on her 60th Birthday

Anuradha of Chennai says that she had wished to go to Shirdi on her 60th birthday and had constantly been praying to Baba to make it happen. She mentioned it casually to her family members and her elder brother made it happen. "It was the most precious gift that I had ever received on any of my birthdays" says Anuradha with a heart filled with emotions.

"I prayed to Baba to bless me with his Udi on my 60th birthday. When we reached Shirdi, we had a wonderful and heart fulfilling darshan of Sai Baba standing close to His Samadhi from where Baba was clearly visible. I couldn't believe that I am in Shirdi as per my wish on my 60th birthday" she said passionately.

"When I received an udi packet at the prasad counter, I requested for one more. I was told only one packet is given per person. Downhearted, I moved forward. The moment I reached the exit gate, I saw an udi packet lying on the ground. I picked it up and happily showed it to all the sai sewaks distributing udi and prasad that Baba himself has given me udi." This incident is viewed by her as a blessing from Baba specially on her 60th birthday as per her wish as the udi packet could have been picked up by anyone, why only her. She had no words to explain her state of mind and she was full of praise for Baba.

A little ahead of the place where she was standing, a lady was distributing chocolates and Anuradha also received one chocolate. Also received the prasad distributed after arathi at a time when the prasad plate was about to finish. The series of incidents that happened on her birthday had further deepened her bond with Baba.

Madhavi delivered a boy

Madhavi of Hyderabad says that she had a lot of issues with her in-laws as a result of which she and her husband had to stay in a separate house independently. Madhavi delivered a girl child. Her mother-in-law always expressed her displeasure to Madhavi for not having delivered a boy. She therefore prayed to Baba and started a 9-weeks fast asking Baba to help her deliver a boy child so that she could be relieved of her mother-in law's verbal abuses and bickering. When Madhavi became pregnant for the second time, she continued to pray to Baba to help her deliver a boy. She was ultimately blessed with a son and Madhavi felt relieved.

Daughter in law conceived

M Srividya of Delhi says that her house owner had a cow shed. One of the cows was pregnant. One day everyone in her landlady's house went out. At that very moment the cow was ready to deliver. She immediately called her landlady but by that time they had gone a little far and were not in a position to return immediately. However, they sent their veterinarian immediately. It was a Friday and a cow delivering on a Friday, being very auspicious, Srividya prayed to Baba for her daughter-in-law to conceive at the earliest. And her daughter in law became pregnant the next month after her prayer. She said that she had no words to thank Baba as he had always been there to help her and fulfill her wishes.

Got a house of choice with Baba's grace

M Srividya of Delhi says that her son's office shifted to another premises within Delhi. In order to reduce the time spent on commuting, they decided to look for a house closer to his office. However, despite their best efforts, they could not find a suitable house within their rental ceiling.

Having lost hopes of getting a good house, dejected, they were returning home. On the way back, there was a huge traffic jam and they were stuck. Just in front of them they saw a "TO LET" board and they got down to give it a try instead of waiting in the traffic jam. To their surprise the house was good, big and beautiful and was far less than their rental ceiling. In front of the house was a big Shiva temple and Baba's statue was also there. Srividya, with her eyes full of tears of joy and heart full of gratefulness to Baba says, "it seems Baba is telling me that "I am protecting you by staying near you".

Bow to Shri Sai
Peace be to all

CHAPTER 3

BLESSED DURING THE FIRST VISIT TO SHIRDI

Anuradha blessed and accepted by Baba on her first visit to Shirdi

Anuradha says, "I went to Shirdi for the first time in May 2003 along with my brother who funded the entire trip. At that time, though I believed in Baba, I was not a staunch devotee as I am now. As we approached the Samadhi Mandir in the queue suddenly a garland fell on my neck. The security guards who were standing on both sides were throwing the garland kept at Baba's feet towards the devotees. I was extremely happy and felt that Baba had accepted me as his devotee and was blessing me. From then onwards My love and faith for Baba began to grow. Even today I have preserved the dry powder of that garland."

Next day in Shaneshwara temple, a person dressed like Baba, standing in one corner of the temple, signalled her to come. When they went to him, he applied Udi on Anuradha's forehead and said in Hindi, *"Ab se tera sab kasht door hoga"* (from now onwards all your sufferings will come to an end). She was very happy on hearing this and paid her respects to him by touching his feet and came out. Suddenly, a thought arose in her mind that he could be Baba himself and hence she went again to see him at the same place within a few seconds. But he was not there. She searched everywhere but he was not found.

Anuradha feels grateful to her brother who took her to Shirdi. She says, "it seems Baba had specially arranged this visit for me to guide me in the right direction. I feel truly blessed."

Baba gave darshan and prasad unexpectedly

V. Sri Vidya Lakshmi of Mumbai who has faith in Baba since her childhood decided to go to Shirdi along with her one-and-a-half year old son with the consent of her husband and booked tickets by a night bus. However, a day before departure her husband said he would also accompany her to Shirdi as going alone with a small kid would be very difficult. Her heart sank fearing if her husband didn't get a seat in the bus, he may ask her also to cancel her trip. But to her surprise, when she called travel agents, they accommodated her husband against a passenger who had just then cancelled his ticket.

Baba's temple was overcrowded when they reached and there was a waiting time of 7-8 hours in the queue for Baba's darshan. Her husband told that it is not practical to wait for such a long time in the queue with a small kid and they were about to leave. With a broken heart and tearful eyes she took some mud from Shirdi soil and applied it on her head while questioning Baba as to why she was not allowed to have His darshan on her first visit? As they were about to leave one lady on her own told Srividyalakshmi that she has a VIP pass for 8 persons but only two have come and that since she is with a small kid, she asked her also to join. With VIP passes they skipped the long queue and directly reached the Samadhi Mandir within less than half an hour. She felt blessed. They had a heart satisfying darshan and after that they went to a restaurant to have lunch. At the restaurant one person dressed like 'dwarpal' of Samadhi Mandir approached them carrying a big communal plate with remnants of mixed dal, rice, veg, etc. and offered them a little bit of mixed baath from the plate and said that he had just then offered this as prasad to Baba. He gave prasad only to them and did not give it to anyone else in the restaurant.

Sri Vidya Lakshmi says, even today when she recollects this incident her eyes become wet and have goosebumps all over. Srividyalakshmi's faith in Baba increased manifold and she realised that Baba would never let his true devotees leave with a heavy heart from Shirdi.

Miracles of Arathi Mohan on her first visit to Shirdi

Arathi Mohan from Karnataka had the good fortune of visiting Shirdi for the first time as part of a 30-devotee team from Vallabha Bhajan Mandali for performing bhajans in Samadhi Mandir on 9th March

2020, on the auspicious occasion of Holi. She very fondly shares her evergreen memories of her first visit.

1) The team had taken Chikki (groundnut burfi) to offer to Sai Baba. She was entrusted with the task of distributing prasad. To her surprise, not only the visitors to the temple, but the priests also partook prasad from her. She considered it as a blessing of Baba as generally the priests don't ask for prasad.

2) Later during the day, Arathi and a few of her friends had the good fortune to visit the Samadhi Mandir where they witnessed Shej arathi, which is possible only through online booking. Arathi says, "we were blessed, I thought. The positive vibrations of a team of 6 young persons performing Sai bhajans at that time permeated the whole temple premises and I immediately reverentially offered the Chikki prasad in recognition of their wonderful service to Baba. Later on, one of the youth gave me a cloth that was used to wipe the face of Baba before performing Arti. The cloth was smeared with sandalwood paste and I was so overwhelmed to get such an invaluable gift." Aarti, with tears of joy flowing down her eyes, said that she has preserved the cloth in her jewel box. She says even today when she opens her almirah the nice aroma of sandal wood

lingers in the entire room. She feels the presence of Baba in that sandalwood aroma.

3) On their way to Shirdi, she received a call from one of her friends and when informed that she is going to Shirdi, he requested her to offer Rs 200/- as Annadaan and immediately transferred the money electronically.

After Shej Arti Arathi says "we met one old man in the temple who was meditating there. One of my friends gave him Rs. 200. Instead of accepting the money he asked for chikki which I was carrying. After offering chikki as requested by him, I offered Rs. 200 and told him 'Khana Kha leejiye Baba'. He immediately accepted it and I felt blessed as a while ago, my friend's offer of Rs 200 was not accepted by him. I also told him that Rs 200 is my friend's contribution and he also blessed my friend."

Later when she messaged her friend about the incident, he replied that he received intimation from Baba around 11.30 p.m. that his annadaan offering was received. She was speechless as exactly that was the time she gave Rs 200 to the old man in the temple.

4) After coming out of Samadhi Mandir, her brother was explaining about the Mandir

and surrounding areas as they were new to the temple. While we were near the place of various deities, a man (of the age of her father when she lost him), dressed like Baba in saffron clothes approached Aarti. She offered respect to him with folded hands. He gave her a chocolate and blessed her and asked her to always maintain her innocent and child-like smile. She didn't see him after that.

All these incidents had created positive vibrations and made an everlasting impression in Arathi's mind. She went back with lots of good memories and with a feeling of being blessed by Baba.

Sripriya's first contact with Baba and her first visit to Shirdi

Sripriya of Chennai says that she did not know anything about Sai Baba till her marriage. She came to know through her mother-in-law's friend when they visited her. After returning home she shared her special experience on Baba with her sister-in-law. Her sister-in-law, being a Baba devotee, gave her Sri Sai Satcharitra and told that reading Satcharitra within a week is very auspicious. At that time she was in acute depression and though she read the entire book in a week only two lines in chapter 2, i.e., **"Hearing my stories and teachings will create faith in devotees' hearts and they will easily get self realisation and bliss"** and the story about

Saibaba returning to Shirdi with Chand Patil was fixed in her mind. She also had the good fortune to watch Saibaba teleserials for the first time, which helped her gain more knowledge about Baba.

Being told by her sister-in-law that if one lights two lamps in front of Baba it would bring good fortune to the family, she stealthily bought a very small statue of Baba and two small earthen lamps while fearing that her family being very orthodox, may not allow her to worship Saibaba. She started lighting lamps in front of Baba daily.

One day she asked her husband to take her to a close by Baba temple. However, when they went the temple was closed. She felt very unfortunate that she couldn't have Baba's darshan. But to her surprise, while returning she saw a hawker selling Baba statues on the pavements and one bright orange coloured statue impressed her most. Though she wanted to buy the same, she didn't have the courage to ask her husband. On return before entering her house she saw some bright colours in her neighbour's house and being attracted by that she asked what it was. Her neighbour told her that it is the statue of Baba - exactly like the one she saw a while ago - and immediately gifted the statue to her as she liked it. Receiving Baba's statue, which she was longing for, she felt very happy.

One day she saw an advertisement regarding Shirdi Yatra. She asked her husband if she can go to

Shirdi, and to her surprise he immediately booked her tickets and also said that she can leave the child with his mother. At that time she was not brave enough to travel alone and no one was there to accompany her to the railway station. On the day of her trip, as soon as she stepped out of her house she saw Baba photo, idol, etc. everywhere. She managed to get into a bus and reached the station just a few minutes ahead of its departure. Coming alone for the first time, she had to find out where and which platform to board the train. Luckily she found her train and got into the train and was shocked when the TTE told her, "Madam, you have come, you are lucky today the train is delayed by 15 minutes" and guided her to the coach reserved for Shirdi devotees.

Sripriya says she never thought that she would visit Shirdi. She says, her husband booking tickets; mother-in-law accepting to take care of her child; permitting to visit Shirdi; not missing the train despite reaching late; seeing Baba everywhere; etc. seemed to be a miracle for her, which she could not even have dreamed of.

Needless to mention, she had a good darshan of Baba in Shirdi and became a very staunch devotee of Baba.

Acquiring own house after first visit to Shirdi

In May 2015 Jayaraman wished to go to Shirdi with his family. However, the train tickets were waitlisted. On the recommendation of a VIP, he got confirmed tickets for the onward journey to Shirdi. However, the return journey tickets remained waitlisted. Therefore his wife and daughter told him to proceed alone, so that no difficulty arises on the return journey in case the tickets are not confirmed.

He went to Shirdi alone and had a wonderful darshan. He was lodged comfortably and went to Shani Signapur and other temples nearby. After his successful Shirdi trip when he went to the station, he found his return tickets were still waitlisted. However, he got into his compartment and occupied a seat. During the entire journey from Nashik to Calicut he travelled comfortably without any disturbance by his co-passengers or the TTE. However his co-passengers were asked to leave the compartment as they had no confirmed tickets. In Goa, one of the passengers offered him two confirmed tickets which he didn't need. He thought in his mind that his daughter and wife also could have accompanied him, as he felt that Baba had already arranged seats for their comfortable return journey.

Jayaraman says, within 15 days of his return from Shirdi, he purchased a house in Calicut.

Bow to Shri Sai
Peace be to all

CHAPTER 4

VARIOUS DISEASES CURED

Rare eye infection cured

Rani Ravi from Chidambaram says that around 15 years back she had a constant itching in her eyes for which she consulted a local doctor, who told her that she had a viral infection similar to chicken pox in the eyes. On being asked if her eye problem is curable, the doctor told her that she needs to consult an ophthalmologist as she has eye chicken pox, which affects the vision as well and further added that everything is in the hands of God. She was very much scared and was worrying about her eye condition. Rani Ravi constantly prayed to Baba to cure her.

She shared this with her Guru, whom she reverentially follows. Her Guru immediately got an appointment fixed with a renowned ophthalmologist in Chennai. It's not easy to get an appointment with that ophthalmologist and one has to wait for more than a week or 10 days to get an appointment with that ophthalmologist but on the intervention of her Guru she got it out of turn for the very next day.

Next day, she reached the hospital exactly at the appointed time when her name was being announced by the office of ophthalmologist. If she had been a little late she would have missed her appointment. At the entrance of the doctor's waiting room, she saw a big photo of Sai Baba and was very pleased to know that the ophthalmologist was also a staunch devotee of Baba. Praying to Baba constantly, she went to meet the doctor.

After examining her eyes the ophthalmologist asked her as to how she noticed her eye problem. She told him that she had a constant itching in her eyes. The ophthalmologist confirmed that she has a kind of viral infection called eye chicken pox which affects one in one lakh persons. He further added that in most of the cases it goes unnoticed and the patients lose their vision. She was very scared to hear all this. She kept praying to Baba asking Him to cure her at the earliest.

The ophthalmologist further said that since she has come at the very initial stages of the infection it is curable. With proper medication and care, within a few weeks her eyes became alright and her faith in Baba increased manifolds. Rani says, if she had not got itching symptoms, she would have not even known about it. She thanked Baba profusely for alerting her with a symptom because of which she could get timely help and cure for her eye chicken pox without losing vision.

Kidney stones cured

Anonymous devotee says "my son who was staying alone was suffering from kidney stones. He was crying out of pain. I asked my sister to take him to a doctor. Simultaneously, I also asked my son to take some udi mixed with water and told him that while passing urine the stones would come out and Baba would surely help you". Her son took udi as advised. Being herself dismayed, as per her usual practice, in the evening she opened a random page from Sri Sai Satcharitra praying Baba to cure her son who is suffering from pains due to kidney stones. To her surprise the page that she opened up was chapter 34 in which a devotee's - Harda gentleman - kidney stones came out while passing urine by intake of udi with water. The moment she finished reading that, she received a call from her son who told her that the stones in the kidney came out while passing urine and in that process he had extreme pain.

Fits cured

Sita of Trichy says that her sister's 2 year old grandson was admitted in the hospital as he had fits. Her sister called her crying and asked her to pray for his quick recovery. As per her practice while praying she opened a random page from Sri Sai Satcharitra. Surprisingly, the page opened was chapter 26 in which Mr. Harishchandra Pitale's son was cured of epilepsy. Immediately she informed her sister about this and asked her to have faith in Baba and that her grandson would be cured soon. And Sita's faith in Baba was reaffirmed when her sister's grandson returned home fully cured.

Knee surgery, the only remedy

Rajeswari of Vijayawada had severe pains in her knees in the year 2016 and was unable to walk which made her feel depressed. Doctors said that more than 75% of her bones have degenerated and her condition was in the third stage for which knee surgery was the only option.

At this very moment, her in-laws planned a pilgrim trip to Gangapur Dattatreya temple and a few other holy places where a holy dip is considered very auspicious by the Hindus. She also wanted to go but her husband told her to relax in her parents house while they go on the pilgrimage and return. She had no choice but to accept.

On the day of their tour Rajeswari accompanied them till the railway station from where she was to reach her mother's house. At this moment her mother-in-law asked her also to accompany and further added that if she is unable to walk she can relax there instead of relaxing here. She was not prepared for the visit. She didn't have any change of clothes etc. However, as she was blessed by Baba everything was arranged and she proceeded with them. To the surprise of all, she walked for miles and miles without the least problem and had a wonderful darshan of all the deities. Since she was feeling better, she did not go for knee replacement surgery as advised by her doctor. After 5 years, today Rajeswari is fine and is walking alright without any knee surgery.

Sanjay's daughter COVID positive after 20 days of delivery

Sanjay Wagh of Aurangabad says that his daughter was tested positive for COVID after 20 days of delivering the child. He constantly prayed to Baba to cure his daughter at the earliest. Sanjay Wagh requested for home isolation treatment by assuring the doctor to undertake all COVID protocol measures. Fortunately, the doctor allowed home isolation and in due course his daughter was cured and the baby also remained safe. Sanjay says that their faith in Baba played a pivotal role in bringing the situation under control

Baba averted Sanjay's knee surgery

In the year 2017, when Sanjay Wagh was riding in his motorcycle, suddenly a dog came in from and he lost balance and fell down. He had a heavy injury in his knees and the reports of the MRI, X-Ray confirmed that a knee surgery is a must and doctors asked him to get admitted immediately.

Sanjay Wagh did not want to go for surgery as that would mean 2-3 months rest in bed and he couldn't afford that being the only breadwinner of the family. However, he started taking the medicines prescribed by the doctors. He also consulted a few more doctors regarding the necessity of a surgery. All of them confirmed that surgery is inevitable.

He went to Shirdi and cast lots at the Samadhi Mandir of Sai Baba asking Baba whether to get the surgery done or not. And he was prepared to act as per Baba's advice. Baba's decision was "no need of surgery" and he did not perform surgery at all. He says now it is about 3 and a half years since this accident and he is walking normally and feeling healthy without knee surgery.

Bow to Shri Sai
Peace be to all

CHAPTER 5

VARIOUS DISEASES CURED - CONTINUED

Blood tests normal

Lalitha from Bengaluru went for a CA 125 blood test in March 2019 and the range was very high and therefore the doctor advised her to repeat the test after 2 months. He further added that if the range continues to be high even after the second report, a surgery would become inevitable. She was extremely worried as she lacked the courage to undergo surgery.

In the meantime one of her friends asked her to read Sri Sai Satcharitra regularly and told that Baba will cure. Having lost all hopes, she turned to Baba to save her from the surgery and started reading Sri Sai Satcharitra regularly.

The wonder of wonders, when she went again in June 2019 along with her second blood test report, the doctor told her that everything was normal. She was overwhelmed and couldn't control her tears of joy flowing down.

Shyamala's diseases cured

Shyamala of Hyderabad was taking 16 pills daily for different health issues. Suddenly, she had a problem in her heart and an angiogram had to be done. Before going for the angiogram she prayed to Baba and asked Him, "why are you testing me so much; why are you increasing my medicines?"

She went to her doctor with her angiogram report. Looking at the report the doctor exclaimed, "it's a miracle! All your problems have dissolved" and he immediately cut down 8 medicines from her regular prescription.

I am sure readers can imagine the plight of Shyamala better than what I could describe.

Shyamala's hip pain cured

In the year 1999 Shyamala of Hyderabad had a severe hip pain and was not even able to walk. She was literally crawling at that time. Doctors said that a surgery has to be done and before that advised an MRI scan. When she went for the scan, after fixing plastic coils around her hips the table started sliding into the machine. At this juncture she started shouting and crying and said she cannot go for an MRI scan. Looking at her behaviour, her aunt who accompanied her scolded her saying, "don't you have brains. MRI is a must. You are a mother of two kids. Is this the way to cry and shout?" While her aunt was scolding she kept on praying to Baba to cure her without an MRI. At that time a senior doctor came to the room and said in a very friendly tone, "don't worry, I will perform the operation without an MRI".

On the day of her surgery, her father requested the doctor to cure Shyamala without a surgery. He also said that he will take her to Hyderabad and take care of her. Then the doctor gave local anesthesia and also an injection. After this she was able to walk. Then she went to Hyderabad. In Hyderabad she took treatment in a nature care hospital and got well. "Baba heard my prayers and sensed my fear for surgery and cured me in a natural way" says Shyamala with a smiling face and a cheerful mood.

Baba cured Bhargav's mother

Bhargav from Vijayawada says that when he was 11 years old, his mother was admitted in JIPMER hospital in Pondicherry for treatment of a serious heart problem, which she had since her pregnancy. The doctors informed that there are only 10% chances of her survival. He prayed to Baba in front of His idol at home to take care of his mother and bring her back home hale and hearty. In Pondicherry when his mother was undergoing surgery almost all the doctors in the operation theatre confirmed that his mother was breathing her last few breaths. His father was panic struck.

At this time, one senior doctor from Punjab, Dr. Singh, was on a visit to JIPMER Pondicherry. While he was taking a round of the hospital, he saw Bhargav's father looking pale sitting in front of the operation theatre. On enquiry he came to know about the critical condition of the patient and immediately went into the operation theatre and did not come out for 6 hours. After 6 hours, Dr. Singh came with a smiling face and announced that the operation was successful.

Bhargav says, "Doctor Singh was a visiting doctor, he didn't know my mother's case history. Still he went into the operation theatre and understanding the case helped my mother come back to life. At that time, even as a child of 11 years, I was sure that it was Baba who visited in the form of Dr. Singh on that day to save my mother. How could Baba not listen to the cries of a young boy" asks Bhargav narrating his miracle

Uttering Sai's name constantly saved the son of Durga

Durga of Aurangabad says that her 15 year old son suffered from a sudden acute pain in his stomach while playing. This happened during the lockdown period. She had to take her son immediately to the local hospital where she was told that her son needs to be taken to a better hospital with more facilities to enable him to be cured of his medical condition. The whole night she kept praying to Baba to cure her son without having the necessity to go to a far away hospital as it would be difficult for her, being a single parent, to travel a long distance leaving her younger son at home. Next day, to her surprise when the doctors saw her son's reports, they told her that her son's condition was improving and there was no need to take him to a bigger hospital. Durga says "uttering Baba's name is magical and does away with all our problems. He is our saviour."

Rajiv Bagga cured

Rajiv Bagga says once he was struggling hard to make his career as a civil contractor and was continuously suffering from losses. One day while in office, he got so stressed out that he felt that his left side became numb and his left hand started shaking. At that time he saw the picture of Baba kept on his table and immediately he felt the paralytic attack subsiding.

Same night while sleeping he felt someone moving his fingers on his heart in circular motion. When he woke up he saw no one around. However he says that after that day he never suffered any heart problems.

Bow to Shri Sai
Peace be to all

CHAPTER 6

VARIOUS DISEASES CURED - CONTINUED

This chapter continues with the stories of various devotees whose ailments were cured just by praying to Baba.

The unforgettable miracle

Lakshmi Kartik of Chennai narrates unforgettable miracle. This happened 7-8 years before when her son was suffering from a cold and they took him to the doctor. On examining her son, the doctor prescribed blood tests, X-Ray, scan, etc. They were wondering why there are so many tests for a common cold? Still they got all the tests done. Before going to the hospital with the reports, they went to Baba temple where she cried in front of Baba fearing what the doctor would say on seeing the reports. She prayed to Baba that nothing serious should be there. She believed that her firm faith in Baba will not let anything serious happen to her son.

The doctor after seeing the reports said that though the blood test is negative, the X-Ray and scan reports show some fungus-like white substance in the throat and if left without treatment will spread to the face and will become difficult to cure. However, the doctor prescribed some medicines and asked to come again after four days, while adding that he is not certain if the medicines will be effective.

Lakshmi says, “we were tensed up and worried and lost interest in food and drink and were all the time enveloped with fear and sorrow as to what would happen to our son. Tears constantly flowed down from our eyes and me and my husband started crying while tightly hugging our son. My mother in law consoled us and asked us to have firm faith in Baba and not to lose heart and that everything will become alright. My mother in law applied udi all over my son’s body”.

She further adds, “our son was normal and was eating and playing while we were in suspense as to what would happen to our son. Four days passed like four years and on the fifth day with fresh X-Ray reports we left home early so that we could see the doctor first. On our way we went to the Baba temple and prayed to Baba with tear-filled eyes and fast heart beats that nothing should happen to our son and to cure him with His miracle. The temple priest also, on seeing our condition, assured us that nothing will happen and that we should trust Baba”.

Then they went to the doctor, with the second X-Ray report. The doctor was looking at the report for about 15 minutes and Lakshmi says, “our condition was terrible during those15 minutes”. After 15 long minutes, the doctor asked us as to why he had asked for an X-Ray. We were shocked to hear this and told him that we did X-Ray as per his advice. The doctor then said, “I don’t see anything in his throat except a little bit of sinus and nothing serious is there". Hearing this Lakshmi says, "both me and my husband were awe-struck and thanked Baba profusely for showering his love on us constantly".

Remembering these unforgettable suspense filled moments they spent during those four days Lakshmi says "Baba first makes us tense and then comforts us. His ways are unique."

Untreated dengue and its side effects

Rajeswari of Vijayawada had dengue in the year 2008 and due to lack of awareness of Dengue at that time the doctor's did not go for any dengue tests. This undiagnosed and untreated dengue had created side effects like GB syndrome, mild paralysis affecting her face and legs. Then she was taken to Hyderabad immediately and consulted a good doctor who diagnosed it as dengue positive and started treatment which lasted for one year including 10 days of hospitalisation.

Even though she has been cured, it affected her nervous system and a lot of side effects had cropped up again. She used to often suffer from dizziness, shoulder pain, body ache, headache, etc. which prevented her from either sitting or standing for a long period of time. She could not talk for more than 10 minutes on the phone. She also had a stressed family life, which further aggravated her condition. She was working as a lecturer in a reputed university but had to quit the job due to health issues.

Fed up of her family issues, one day she prayed to Baba to kindly deviate her attention from the family issues so that she can get some relief. At this moment, she received a call from a stranger asking if she would like to take up some sewa for Baba which she gladly accepted. This involved connecting with people, liaising with them, including talking constantly on phone, etc. Initially she found it to be challenging and dropped out. However, on realising that her psychological condition had improved to a great extent after she started Baba's service, she resumed her services to Baba.

Today Rajeshwari says that she is relaxed and spends her time meaningfully. Her condition has improved so drastically that health issues mentioned above have automatically dissolved. She daily uses udi like medicine to keep her health in tact.

Being a staunch devotee of Baba from her childhood, Rajeswari says, "Baba always thinks about the welfare of his devotees and He knows what to give and when to give".

Santhi's successful surgery

One day while in the market Santhi of Bengaluru was attracted by a small size (but a heavy one) grinding mill in the market. She immediately remembered Baba and his wheat grinding and, being a very staunch devotee of Baba, wanted to have one at her house and hence purchased the same. Since she couldn't find any transport to return home she carried the heavy grinding mill and walked home.

Next day she felt some big lump in her abdomen and little pain. Hence she went to the doctor who after performing the necessary CA 125 test, told her that she has a cyst in her ovary for which a surgery is inevitable as the cyst is big in size. Before the surgery she became very nervous and was also scared about the post surgery biopsy report.

Her surgery was scheduled for November 20, 2021. One day before her delivery she received a Saibaba book, udi, prasad, Baba idol and a night lamp plug with Baba image, which she had requested someone to send. She carried the entire thing to the hospital before the surgery and kept it with her till her return from the hospital.

Her surgery went off well without any physical pain to her and she never felt that she was in the hospital. Her biopsy report was non-cancerous and all other reports were also normal both before and after the surgery.

Santhi says "Baba had really given me a hint about my cyst by making me carry the grinding mill home myself. I would have not known about the cyst, if I got a conveyance back home that day". Looking at the way Baba had arranged the things smoothly, she felt happy and relieved.

Rani Ravi's pain in legs cured miraculously

Rani Ravi of Chidambaram was suffering from severe pain in both her legs. Unable to bear the intolerable pain, she constantly prayed to Baba to cure her. She was not able to walk independently. At that time she came to know that reading Sai Stavana Manjari cures all illnesses. She started listening to Sai Stavana Manjari twice a day - after dinner and before going to sleep. One day while listening to Stavana Manjari she dozed off. She had a dream and in the dream Baba came and gave instructions to lift her leg up, down, sideward, etc. and sometimes He Himself helped her move her legs.

When she woke up in the morning she realised that her pains had subsided and that she was able to walk without any support. She also recollected that she woke up and went to the toilet without any support around 3 a.m. She couldn't control her tears when she remembered her dream vision where Baba gave her instructions and also moved her legs in all directions. She says, true to what I heard, after listening to Sai Stavana Manjari, Baba himself became the doctor and cured me.

In Chapter 3 of Sri Sai Satcharitra Sai Baba says, "**If My stories are listened to, all the diseases will be got rid of.....".** All the stories in Chapters 4-6 are a true illustration of Baba's dictum in the Kaliyug.

Bow to Shri Sai
Peace be to all

CHPATER 7

TIMELY ASSISTANCE

Reached home safe

Santhi of Bengaluru says that while travelling by a cab on a flyover on the highway, a speeding car from behind hit them with force and their car swirled and stopped. However, Santhi, her son and the cab driver were safe and unhurt. The back of the car was totally smashed and Santhi and her son were in a state of shock. However, they felt relieved to see that the car swirled in the same spot and did not skid, in which case the car could have fallen down smashing the railings of the flyover, which could have been fatal.

Being on the highway there was no network and they couldn't book another cab. It was night time and raining and none of the passers by stopped. Santhi repeatedly prayed to Baba to help them reach home safely. Suddenly to their surprise, a passing Ola cab offered to drop them home. Thanking Baba, they boarded the vehicle and reached home. The cab driver refused to take money. However they inserted Rs. 200 in his shirt pocket as he continuously refused to take money.

In hindsight, Santhi could make out that Baba was there with them throughout their journey and it was Baba who dropped them home as the cab drivers generally charge double the meter amount to drop home at night time and more if it rains heavily.

Baba coming as cab driver

Jyothi of Chennai had booked a cab from Kodambakkam to her residence, but had to wait for more than half an hour for the cab to reach the spot. When she boarded the cab, the driver told her that the fan belt is broken and the car may stop any time. Hearing this Jyothi told him to keep uttering "Baba" and they will reach their destination. He gazed at her and started driving. Just 2-3 kms before her house the cab driver asked her to get down. Jyothi pleaded to drop her home as her house was not very far from that place. To this the cab driver retorted, "if I utter Baba, the cab may reach your house but then I will have to carry the car on my head. The workshop is here, please let me fix my cab and you take another vehicle". She had to get down. Due to poor network she couldn't book another cab and requested the cab driver to help her in booking another cab.

Within a few minutes an auto came in front of her and the driver offered to drop her to her destination. His proactive offer made Jyoti doubt him and she politely refused saying that she is booking another cab. A stranger who was standing adjacent to her told her that not a single vehicle had come that day in that area and hence she should proceed with that auto. Hearing this, she looked around, and realised that the roads were deserted. Doubting that they could be conspiring against her, she again refused to take the auto. However, the auto driver insisted and the cab driver also advised her to take the auto. Unwillingly and fearfully she boarded the cab and silently uttered Baba's name to reach her destination safely.

To her surprise, suddenly the auto driver (as though he heard her repeating "Baba" constantly) said, "can't you believe me when you are uttering Baba's name constantly?' Being shocked she was groping for a reply when the auto driver told her that, "every Thursday at 3 a.m I deliver flowers for decoration to the temple deity in Mylapore". Hearing this she thought for a second that Baba himself is travelling with her but dismissed the idea. On reaching her destination she asked him as to which auto stand he belongs to. He said that he is from one of the nearby auto stands. She paid the auto driver and went home.

Sometime later, while recollecting the above episode, out of curiosity she tried to find out about the auto driver who dropped her on that day. When she enquired with two three auto stands about the auto driver, no one could recognise him.

Jyothi says that during the two years of her stay there she had never seen that auto driver ever before or after. It was then that she realised that

Baba had come to her rescue on the day when she needed a vehicle badly.

Baba - The Wirepuller

Purnima from Vellore says, "both me and my husband were hospitalised on March 18, 2021 after being tested positive for COVID and were discharged on March 22, 2021. I was just looking for someone who would supply food at home as being weak, I knew I would not be able to cook. I had messaged on Facebook and few people responded. However, only one lady named Bhuvana agreed knowing that we were COVID patients".

When she saw Sai Baba on Bhuvana's facebook display picture, Purnima felt that Baba had come to her rescue. She then called Bhuvana and requested her to get her Baba's udi along with dinner. She said she didn't have udi at home. However, when she opened the dinner box, she found a packet of udi. Later she found out that Bhawana specially went to a nearby Baba temple, prayed for them and got udi from the temple. Medicines coupled with Udi and her faith in Baba cured them completely of COVID within a few days.

'"Baba would cross seven seas to protect His devotees", says Purnima filled with devotion and love for Baba. Today, Bhuvana visits her house often and they have become good friends.

Baba's timely monetary assistance

Amrita Pandey of Faridabad narrates her unforgettable experience with Baba, which according to her, is nothing less than a miracle. She shares an incident that took place when their financial condition was not good. They were finding it difficult to make both ends meet. It was month-end and she didn't have a single penny with her. At this time her husband asked for Rs. 200 which she couldn't give. In his desperation, her husband asked her to check again. Being helpless, she looked at Baba's photo in the kitchen, and asked him, " how can I get Rs. 200? Please help". At this very moment the doorbell rang and her neighbour came in with a box of sweets, marriage invitation card and Rs. 200 for inviting them for her daughter's wedding. She said she couldn't purchase chocolates for her daughters and asked her to purchase the same with Rs. 200. "I was stupefied and didn't know if I should thank Baba first or ask my neighbour to sit" said Amrita.

With tears of joy in her eyes Amrita says, Baba reads the minds of His devotees and fulfils their needs.

Jayaraman's daughter cured

Jayaraman of Kerala says he was a devotee of Satya Sai Baba. He was in the process of finding a good hospital / doctor for the heart and eye operation for his daughter. The quotes received from various hospitals were around Rs. 3.5 lakhs and involved a very lengthy procedure. At this time he heard about Shirdi Sai Baba and started praying to Baba to help him cure his special needs daughter at the earliest.

Through one of his friends he came to know that the Central Institute of Trivandrum performs such surgeries for as less as Rs. 50,000. When he went to Trivandrum, he came to know that there was a scheme under which special needs children are provided treatment free of cost. Immediately, he started the treatment for his daughter which was carried out successfully. Within a month his daughter recovered completely. Jayaraman says, "I have no words to thank Baba who arranged everything for me smoothly and free of cost. It's a miracle that I can never forget in my life" says Jayaraman.

Marital issues resolved

Bhargav and his wife had many differences of opinion and he feared that this may affect his child's development. His wife went to her parents house. His constant efforts to bring her back did not yield any result. Again, as usual he prayed to Baba to resolve the marital issues and bring back his wife. While no one was able to convince his wife to return with him, the cab driver - whom he engaged to and fro for his wife's place - who was also a devotee of

Baba, mediated and amicably resolved the issue in a simple way as Baba does!

Saved from heavy monetary penalty

Kirutika of Dubai says that last year a few families together planned an outing during a weekend to Ras al Khaimah (RAK), in UAE. There, one of their team members was caught by Public Service Department (PSD) personnel of RAK for urinating in public. The person who was caught hinted to the other team members to move away. When questioned by the PSD personnel he said he doesn't know anyone. They even took away his ID card. Kruthika says she was very much tensed up as her team member will be heavily penalised. Kiruthika constantly prayed to Baba to save him and extricate him from this difficult situation. Next day, the team member received a message that he has been penalised with a huge amount of money, which he can't afford. She kept praying to Baba to rescue her him of this great financial hardship.

To her surprise, the very next day they came to know that on the occasion of the National Day of UAE, as per their usual practice, the UAE Government, had provided 'discount' on the penalty. The other team members who were not caught, on moral grounds, came forward to equally share the penalty amount. Thus, the amount payable by the person who was caught was reduced to a reasonable amount.

Kiruthika thanked Baba profusely for this timely assistance.

Baba came to the rescue of Abhishek

Abhishek of Vijayawada, a young and an ardent devotee of Baba, keeps performing a lot of charitable works. Once he and his friends went to distribute food to poor and needy people which was around 20 kms away from the place of his stay. By the time they finished, it was almost 9:30 p.m. and they were about to leave. At that time a very poor lady, who was very weak and unable to stand and shivering, came asking for food. They provided food to her. But, she being weak, was not in a position to eat the food herself. Having sympathy on her condition, Abhishek sat beside her and started feeding her. His friends kept on insisting him to leave and pack up as they were getting late. Whereas, Abhishek told them just to wait for another 15-20 minutes so that the lady finishes her food and they can leave. However, without waiting for Abhishek his friends left the place. After feeding the poor lady when Abhishek left he couldn't get a bus. A few more others were also waiting for the bus to come. The time was ticking by and it was past 11 p.m. Abhishek was worried as his father would scold him if he goes late and he constantly kept praying to Baba to help him reach home safe. At that time, a truck came and stopped in front of Abhishek and asked him where he was bound to. Abhishek wondered why the vehicle stopped only in front of him and not others present.

Further, he was also scared that they may charge a lot of money as he had only a few rupees for the bus fare. He made it clear to the truck driver that had no money to pay him except the bus fare. The truck driver dropped him near his house without any charges.

He said that at that late hour a truck coming and giving him a free ride upto his house is beyond his imagination. "I am sure it was Baba who came to my rescue that night," said Abhishek.

Saibaba says in Chapter 40 of Sri Sai Satcharitra, **"I always think of him who remembers Me. I require no conveyance, carriage, tanga, nor train nor aeroplane. I run and manifest myself to him who lovingly calls me."** The stories of this chapter are a true manifestation of the above dictum of Baba.

Bow to Shri Sai
Peace be to all

CHAPTER 8

VOWS FULFILLED

Ovarian cysts dissolved

Dr. Sneha of Hyderabad was diagnosed with polycystic ovary syndrome (PCOS) with a large cyst in her left ovary. Her doctor suggested surgery. She was very much worried. One day (Thursday) when she was driving, she saw the vehicle of Sai Baba Bhajan Group in front of her car. Immediately, she prayed to Baba to pop her cysts just like a water bubble and also vowed to Baba that if that really happens she will read his Holy book Sri Sai Satcharitra and also observe fasting for 5 Thursdays. After this she went to the radiologist. When the radiologist was testing her stomach she felt like her cyst was popping out. The doctor was astonished. Dr. Sneha says, "I myself being a doctor never believe in such miracles but after my own experience I not only believe in divine miracles, but also became a staunch devotee of Baba and started reading Sri Sai Satcharitra regularly."

Got the prasad and broke the fast

Srividhya of New Delhi fasted for 13 Thursdays and every Thursday she used to go to Baba temple to break the fast with Baba's prasad. On the last Thursday of her fasting, after Baba's darshan, she stood in the queue for the prasad. Everyone before her got the prasad and exactly when it was her turn prasad finished. She repeatedly pleaded to the temple authorities to give her a tiny amount of prasad stuck to the plate, but they replied that they had already washed the plates.

She was dismayed for not being able to break her last day's fast and started returning when someone from behind called her by tapping her shoulder. When she turned, a tall well built lady in white saree with a big bindi and red blouse, offered her prasad in both her hands in two disposable bowls.

She had her prasad and searched for the lady in the entire temple, but could not find her. Srividhya says that "Baba would never let his devotee go hungry come what may. He would ensure that His devotees fulfill their religious vows observed by them".

Strange message from the son

Nageshwara Rao of Vijayawada was working with a chit fund company. He was entitled to a handsome incentive, if he achieved the target set. He therefore constantly prayed to Baba to help him achieve the target and also mentally vowed that if he did achieve the target and receive the incentive, he would set aside Rs 10,000 for Baba. With the blessings of Baba he did achieve his target and did get his incentive and kept aside Rs. 10,000 to be given to Baba on his next visit to Shirdi.

After about 2-3 months, during the Dussehra period, he needed some money urgently and hence he took out Rs. 10,000/- kept separately for Baba, thinking that he would soon replace it. After a few days, when Nageshwara Rao was in his office, he received a message on his phone from his 10 year old son which read as: "You have used Rs. 10,000 kept for buying toys for me. Tomorrow I am going to die.". Shocked to see this message, Nageshwara Rao rushed home to see what the matter was but his son was normal and he never mentioned anything about his toys, etc. His son also did not remember what message he sent to his father except that he sent something but didn't know what.

At that time Nageshwara Rao realised his mistake of utilising the money earmarked for Baba and also realised the significance of the message as the next day was Vijayadashami, Baba's punyatithi. Needless to say, having taken the hint from the message, Nageshwara fulfilled his vow without any further delay.

Reinstated in job

Ritu from Rajasthan says that her father was deprived of his job 18 years ago and had a very tough time facing his friends and relatives. All their efforts to get him reinstated met with a dead end. At this time, Ritu started 51 weeks of Sai Baba Thursday fasting. On the 11th week of her fasting, her father was reinstated with full honour. During this period, Ritu also got her first job.

"Baba heard my prayer and blessed my father to regain his lost job. His 18 years of suffering had ended and I have nothing more to ask for" says Ritu emotionally.

Mother's health condition improved

Bhargav of Vijayawada says he got engaged in March 2018 (Thursday) and got married in May 2018 (Thursday). Immediately after the marriage, they went to Annavaram for the darshan of Lord Satyanarayana Swamy. His mother also went with them. There his mother fainted and was hospitalised. Bhargav was very much worried and prayed to Baba to cure his mother at the earliest, as any untoward incident immediately after the marriage will not be considered as a good omen. He also made a vow to Baba that if his mother recovers, he will visit Shirdi with his wife. Two hours after Bhargav's prayers to Baba, his mother recovered. As per his promise, Bhargav went to Shirdi with his wife. Bhargav considers this episode as Baba's plan to bring him and his wife to Shirdi immediately after their marriage for seeking His blessings.

Seven week's parayan yielded results

An ardent Sai devotee Sandhya says that when her parents visited a Saibaba temple in their hometown, the priest had told her father, "ask your daughter to read Sri Sai Satcharitra Parayan for 7 weeks. It will do her good". As per her father's advice, she started her Parayan with the blessings of Baba. She also decided to keep aside dakshina of Rs. 1000 every week as annadaan for the poor and needy.

At this time, one of her friends was raising funds for his colleague's mother who was undergoing brain surgery. Thinking that helping someone in need is as good as annadaan, she donated 6 weeks' parayan dakshina Rs. 6000 to this noble cause.

After 2 weeks of Parayan, she says, "there was a difference in the way I was reading Sri Sai Satcharitra. Every week there was a change in me and when I read Sri Sai Satcharitra I used to cry, sob, quiver and get goosebumps etc. while reading the stories. The Parayan made me more disciplined in my personal life. Further, I realised that the way I was doing Parayan was far different than the previous Parayans. My concentration power increased and I was understanding every word of what I was reading."

Sandhya says "I always used to wonder why miracles don't happen in my life when so many devotees experience miracles. During the 7th week of parayan my mother told me that a saint visited her house with a picture of Sai Baba seeking donation for Annadan. Further the saint said to my mother that 'one of your daughters (that is me) is an ardent devotee of Sai Baba and Sai Baba is always with her.' My mother paid Rs 1000 to him, the same amount that was earmarked as my 7th week's dakshina."

Sandhya says that, "looking in hindsight, I now realise that many miracles did happen in my life also but I never recognised them."

Topped in the school exams

Aishwarya fasted for 9 weeks before her 10th exams praying to Baba to do well in her exams. When the results were announced she was surprised to see that she came not only first in the school but had also secured maximum marks in Mathematics standing first in that subject. Aishwarya says she never expected that she would be the topper of the school and attributes her success to Baba's grace and blessings on her.

Bow to Shri Sai
Peace be to all

CHAPTER 9

EXAMINATIONS CLEARED

Amrita's daughter got admission in Delhi University

When Amrita's daughter was in Grade XII, one of her relatives asked her about the plans for her daughter's higher studies. She replied that she has not thought about it yet. To this, her relative said sarcastically that "you are saying as if your daughter will get 90% marks and will get admission in Delhi University." Amrita kept quiet. She had faith in her daughter's hard work as well as in Baba.

"My daughter appeared in Grade XII and I kept praying to Baba to bless my daughter with 90% as she deserves that. When the results were announced she did secure 90% marks. She did her graduation from Delhi University and is now working in a very good firm. Baba's miracles are endless" says Amrita.

Exams cleared with Baba's grace

V. Sri Vidya Lakshmi of Mumbai says that she had always been a bright student and had been a topper. At the time of her exams, her mother suddenly fell ill and was hospitalised. As a result Sri Vidya Lakshmi could not get enough time to prepare for her third subject. She had already prepared very well for the other two two subjects.

However, she appeared in the exams and performed very well in the two subjects she was prepared for and the third one, according to her, was not upto her mark. However, when the results were declared she had got 65% and 80% in the two subjects she had well prepared and just about 40% (cut off mark for clearing any single paper) in the third subject. Based on the aggregate marks as also single subject cut off, she had cleared her exams successfully. "During those days to score anything around 45-50% marks was considered outstanding" says Sri Vidya Lakshmi.

According to her this is a sheer miracle of Baba, as she never expected to clear her third paper for which she was ill prepared. Attributing her success to Baba's blessings, being a very staunch devotee of Baba from a very young age, she says, "my joy knew no bounds when I saw that I had scored exactly 40% to clear the paper, not one mark less or more. With a cheerful mood and a smile on her face, she said, "Baba never lets his devotees down".

Got admission miraculously

After her schooling, Aishwarya had applied for higher education. She did not get admission as there were no seats available. She prayed to Baba to help her. After some days casually when she went to the college to check if there is a possibility of getting admission, she was overwhelmed to hear that one seat was available for a four year B.Sc. Nursing course. She immediately got herself enrolled for that course. “It seems Baba had specifically reserved one seat for me”, said Aishwarya happily.

During her four years in the college, her first exam alone was on a Thursday and she secured distinction in that subject. All other exams though she did well, she did not get distinction as they were not scheduled on a Thursday. Aishwarya says, “with Baba everything is possible.”

Her experiences with Baba had not only made her a staunch devotee of Baba but also her entire family started believing in Baba. She says if she doesn’t have Baba’s darshan in the morning, her day doesn’t go well.

Bow to Shri Sai
Peace be to all

CHAPTER 10

BLESSED WITH A CHILD

Namita gets the bliss of motherhood with Baba's blessings

Namita from Puri had two consequent miscarriages and was longing for a baby. Third time when she became pregnant her gynaecologist advised her complete bed rest and prescribed injections as the size of the fetus was not satisfactory. She was praying to Baba constantly to bless her with a successful pregnancy and a healthy baby.

Given her past track record, she was full of fear. During her subsequent visit to the gynae she saw a picture of Baba in the clinic. The nurse who administered the injection was wearing a pendant which had Baba's photo. She was happy to see Baba everywhere and thought that Baba is assuring her that He is with her.

During the fourth month of her pregnancy she saw Baba in her dream wearing white Kafni coming near her. Baba lifting the sleeves of His kafni upto elbow put His hand inside her abdomen and was twisting and turning his hands as if He is trying to settle the things inside her. All the while Baba's face was tensed up, she says. After sometime Baba told her, “don’t worry my child, everything is ok now”.

During the sixth month of her pregnancy, she had another dream in which she and her husband were standing at the gate of the Baba temple near her house, where they often used to go. Baba told two of his devotees to take garlands and give them to my “bhakts” who are standing outside the gate. The ladies came and gave garlands to them. After this dream things started improving for her.

At the time of delivery, she says she didn’t have labour pains and doctors suggested induced labour pain, which she did not agree to. She preferred C-section instead. Namita says, “I was filled with fear as I approached Operation Theatre. In the OT, I saw a picture of Baba in the medicine shelf kept near my bed. Baba, my Saviour, reached ahead of me in the OT to ensure smooth delivery”.

She delivered a boy whom they call Sai at home. She says similar miracles happened during her second pregnancy also. Namita, mother of two boys, says that “I have no words to explain the miracles of Baba which turned my life upside down”. Baba is our “maibaap” she says with heartfelt gratitude and complete surrender to Baba.

Conceived after three and a half years

An anonymous devotee says that her daughter did not conceive even after three and a half years of marriage. Her daughter is an ardent devotee of Baba. Though she doesn't get time to read Sri Sai Satcharitra because of her busy schedule in her noble profession, on some Thursdays she tries to read. However, she always speaks to Baba and doesn't start her work in her workplace without first praying to Baba mentally.

They were about to consult a gynaecologist and start treatment for infertility, if any. In the meantime, the anonymous devotee told me with a feeling of gratitude to Baba that her daughter's pregnancy was confirmed. She was sharing this happy news first with me as I was writing the book, even before informing her relatives. The expected delivery date is end May 2022. The devotee has firm faith that Baba will take care of her daughter and her grandchild throughout her daughter's pregnancy and will ensure a smooth and safe delivery and a healthy baby.

Blessed with a baby

Jyothi Suresh of Chennai, an ardent devotee of Baba, says that she had been longing to have a baby. She always prayed to Baba to wash away her sins, if any, and bless her with a kid. She says she often talks to Baba and also could hear Him speak to her. One day in her dream she saw a very very extremely bright light, about 10000 watts, she describes. At that time she was standing near a florist to purchase a rose flower for offering to Baba. Suddenly a palanquin comes and is kept down and Baba signalled to come. Everyone looks behind and she too does the same but no one was behind her. And everybody told her that Baba is calling her. Forgetting the rose flower she went towards Baba. Despite the excess glare, she was able to see Baba clearly but the constant flow of tears obstructed her clear vision. And Jyothi could see Baba sitting in the palanquin and signalling her to come close. She goes towards Baba and sits kneeling down in front of Baba. Though she wished to ask Baba why she is suffering without a child, she was unable to utter a single word. She could hear Baba say “Karma”. Then she felt like asking when she will conceive. Again unable to voice her concern. To this Baba says, “I know what to give and when to give”. She felt happy that knowing her heart Baba answered her queries. At this moment she woke up and realised that it was a dream.

After some days she conceived and delivered a boy. Throughout the time she was in the hospital and while delivering the baby, she held tightly close to her Baba’s key chain. Her husband told her that he had prayed that Baba should be born to them and that he believed that it is Baba who was born to them. On the third day after the baby’s birth she asked Baba if her baby boy is Baba himself. And further prayed to Baba that, "Baba, if it is You who are born to me, then confirm the same in my dream or confirm in the form of a heavy downpour."

Days passed by and they were busy preparing for the celebration of 28th day cradle and naming ceremony of the baby. Suddenly, a day before the ceremony around 4 p.m. it started drizzling and slowly it picked up from heavy to stormy rain. All the arrangements made by them for welcoming the guests for the next day's function got washed away. They were worried about the next day's function as they had already invited a lot of guests. Immediately, they got involved in making alternate arrangements for the next day's function. It rained continuously for 14 hours. When she asked Baba, as to why He is testing them like this, suddenly, a voice in her asked, "have you forgotten?" On hearing this she recollected her prayer to Baba. She burst into tears as Baba had answered her prayers. She was unable to believe that Baba could fulfill the desire of an ordinary person like her. Jyothi says with excitement and gratitude, "the two letter magical word "Baba" will help anyone cross a mountain with ease."

Jyothi says, even today this incident is fresh in her mind and she can never forget this miracle, as it had never happened that it rained so heavily for such a long time and untimely. Needless to say, with Baba's blessings, the rains subsided without any trace of it and the function went off very well to the satisfaction of all. Chapter 40 of Sri Sai Satcharitra says, "**when the devotees surrender themselves completely to their Sadguru, He sees to it that, the religious functions in their houses are duly executed and complied with all the necessary formalities'.** Jyothi's miracle is a true manifestation of this statement.

Jyothi says with uncontrollable tears of joy welled up in her eyes that everything happens with Baba's will. Once we realise this, we can feel Baba's presence every minute in our life. Baba will always ensure the welfare of His devotees and will never ever let down His devotees who not only have unbounded faith but also have completely surrendered to Him.

Conceived after 17 years of marriage

Gomathi and Doraisamy of Perur, Coimbatore, had no issue even after 17 years of their marriage. Their prayers to several Gods and Goddesses did not yield any result. Finally, hearing the fame of Theethipalayam Sai Baba temple, they visited the temple and prayed to Baba for an issue. Gomathi delivered a healthy baby six months back and to mark this joyous occasion as well as to express their heartfelt gratitude to Baba, the couple donated a bag full of rice to the temple.

Conceived after 7 years

Ritu Saxena of Rajasthan says "Since 2008 I am devoted to Baba as if my soul has imbibed his vibes.

Since then I was blessed with each and every wish except motherhood. It's been 7 years of our marriage. My husband is in the merchant navy and therefore I suffered a lot from loneliness and not having a child made me feel depressed as well. Every possible treatment, including two IVFs failed. Then I decided to leave everything to Baba".

"On April 21, 2021, I came to know that I have conceived naturally. On November 25, 2021 (Thursday), I was blessed with a baby. Now I am speechless and have no words to thank Baba, who has fulfilled each and every wish of mine" says Ritu in a merry mood.

Bow to Shri Sai
Peace be to all

CHAPTER 11

IMPROVED ECONOMIC CONDITIONS / LIVING CONDITIONS

Baba's timely financial assistance and financial prosperity

Srividhya of New Delhi says that once when they went to a local vegetable market one person who was selling the photo of Baba came after them and asked them to purchase one picture of Baba. Despite her saying no, he followed her and repeatedly requested her to buy one as it was not very expensive and that he would also earn something to eat. Looking at the beautiful form of Baba, she purchased it. She pasted the picture on a cardboard sheet and hung it on the wall.

At that time they were surrounded by miseries, including financial misery. But immediately after they purchased the picture of Baba, her business prospects started improving slowly. Believing the picture of Baba as a good omen, they decided to get the picture framed and gave it to a local shop. The cost of framing the picture was Rs. 400 and they had paid Rs. 100. From the day they gave the Baba's photo for framing, Srividhya did not receive any business. Her husband was already having some issues with his business partner and their financial situation became worse day by day so much so that they did not have money to have two meals a day.

At this time, suddenly, her husband met an old friend of his who returned Rs. 400 which her husband gave him when his friend was in a financially tough situation. Her husband had totally forgotten about this. Having received this money unexpectedly her husband immediately brought back home Baba's picture duly framed.

Srividhya says the day Baba's picture returned to their house, suddenly she got a call from her friend who gave her business worth Rs 2000 and their financial condition started improving gradually. During those days, Rs. 2000 was a huge amount and Baba made it possible. A family could have two simple meals for the entire month with Rs 2000 during those days, she says. After this incident, Srividhya and her family became a staunch devotee of Baba.

Subsidy approved

Shankar Rajput of Aurangabad says that after he established his tyre business, he constructed a warehouse during the lockdown period and had rented the warehouse to a renowned company. After a few days, when he happened to meet a friend of his, he told him that for the warehouse construction ladies get 35% subsidy, which means he should get around Rs. 50 lakhs. He therefore, approached the concerned authorities seeking subsidy for the warehouse constructed. He was told by the officials there that the subsidy is provided at the time of construction and not after construction and hence he is not eligible for the same. He therefore told Baba to do the best for him as he thinks right.

A few days after this incident he went to Shirdi by foot along with a Palki procession and returned from there on Sunday, November 14, 2021. On November 17, he got a call from the officials at Nashik to come to their office with all the warehouse documents and apply for the subsidy as he got approval from his senior officers for sanction of the subsidy to him. He immediately applied for the same and got a benefit of Rs. 49 lakhs. He was wonderstruck to see how Baba managed his affairs successfully for him.

Kala deserted by her husband

Kala Deshapati of Siddipet, Telengana, got married in 1997 at the age of 18 even before completing her +2 exams. In the year 1999 she delivered a boy. Since her husband was financially supportive of her in her continuing higher education even after marriage, she continued her studies and finished her graduation, double post graduation, etc. She started facing a lot of marital problems and her husband estranged her and stopped supporting her financially. In 2006 she also lost her only son. Till that time she had no faith in God nor believed in God. Suddenly one day, she went to the Sai Baba temple near her house where she received a roti as prasad. This was during the time when she was financially in a very bad shape with no money to eat even a single meal. Then, she started reading Sri Sai Satcharitra as advised by her friend.

One day having been tired of marital problems and also being totally shattered by tragedy faced in her life, she told Baba to kill her husband. She says she can hear Baba talking to her often. When she made this strange request to Baba she could hear Baba telling her, "no my child. Control yourself. It is difficult to lead a life of a widow."

After this she came to terms with life and being herself well educated concentrated on getting a job for herself to remain financially independent. She established a Baba temple at home. Her prospects started improving slowly. She got a job. In the year 2014 there was a rain of Baba's udi in her house continuously for one week and all the people started visiting her house. After this incident, she became a staunch devotee of Baba.

On the second anniversary of the establishment of a temple in her house, she organised a "havan". In the havan fire, Baba appeared.

She says with full contentment that today she lacks nothing. She has a son of 9 years and a daughter of

4 years. She has a house and a car of her own. She is working as a gazetted officer, which she never thought of. All this she attributes to Baba's blessings, Who not only guided her at every stage of life but always protected her with his divine shield.

Srividya's life enriched

M. Srividya of Delhi says her husband was working in a private company with no steady income and she was working as a school teacher. Their financial condition was not at all good, but somehow the education of her son remained unaffected as he got free education in the school where she was working. Once her mother had a problem in her leg and was unable to walk. She used to crawl from one place to another within the house. Since no one was there to take care of her mother, she kept her mother in her house. Her son, who was in 10th standard at that time, secured very poor marks in his exams as he was also taking care of his grandmother who was unable to walk.

Once one of their relatives invited her for the engagement ceremony. And also told her to be present 2-3 hours ahead of the actual ceremony. When she reached their house, her relative was not there. She felt insulted, because it was the usual practice with many of her relatives to ignore her because of her economically weaker condition. However, instead of waiting there till her relative returns, Srividya decided to stroll around the area and return after sometime. While walking through the streets she came across a Saibaba temple. She went in and unaware tears started rolling down her eyes, seeing the wonderful statue of Baba. She also received one "Sai Vrat" book from one of the devotees at the temple. This was her first contact with Baba.

She started her 9 weeks fasting praying to Baba for improvement in her mother's health condition and for her son to get good marks in class X exams. In the 7th week of her fasting her mother's condition improved and she started walking. Then her mother went back to her house. Needless to say her son studied well and completed his +2 examination with good marks.

Her son went to college where he studied well and given his commitment to studies and good grades, the college authorities returned half the tuition fees. He got concessions every time. There was a campus interview in the college. At this time, Srividya heard about saptah reading of Sri Sai Satcharitra. She completed the book in one week praying for her son to get a good placement in the campus interview. Her son got selected in 7-8 companies and he chose to join TCS. He was posted in Bengaluru. Then TCS sent him to their Delhi office. Given his wonderful performance he was posted in Chennai and then to Hyderabad. Looking at his excellent track record, he was then promoted as an Executive in the Financial

Department of TATA SIA Airlines (Vistara). He got married to a very good girl with a 100% matrimonial match.

Srividya relating her life's forward journey with Baba proudly said that today she is a grandmother of a cute baby. Srividya says Baba made her move with high esteem in front of the relatives who once insulted, ignored and disrespected her.

Srividya's miracles are a true example of Baba's dictum in chapter 3 of Sri Sai Satcharitra where Baba says **"If a man utters My name with love, I shall fulfill all his wishes, increase his devotion. And if he sings earnestly My life and My deeds, him I shall beset in front and back and on all sides"**

Moved and settled comfortably in Calicut

Jayaraman of Kerala has witnessed a lot of miracles in his life since the time he started believing in Baba and praying to him. After his daughter's treatment he wished to move to Calicut as he did not receive any support for his special needs daughter in Wayanad.

When he moved to Calicut, he was surprised to see that he got a good house on rent and a good school for his daughter without any great efforts.

He stayed in the rented house from the year 2012 to 2015 peacefully, happily and comfortably. Financially too he was self-sufficient.

Bow to Shri Sai
Peace be to all

CHAPTER 12

Dream come true

Longing desire fulfilled

Arun B Ghodke from Aurangabad reads Sri Sai Satcharitra daily and while reading he used to wonder how nice it would have been if he was with Baba when he was alive and how lucky he would have been to remain closer to Baba's feet.

Once his best friend Bipin Bhau invited him to his house for a religious function. Bipin Bhau is the fifth generation of Baiza Bai's son Tatya Kote Patil. Bipin Bhau had kept in his shrine the wallet which Baba himself made and from which he used to distribute money to various devotees daily from the dakshina collected by Him. Generally, the friends and devotees visiting Bipin Bhau's house used to have a view of the wallet from a distance only. But on that day Bipin Bhau had taken the wallet and gave it in Arun's hand, who was fortunate enough to touch that wallet prepared by Baba with His hands. Arun and others placed some dakshina in the wallet. Suddenly, in front of everyone, Bipin Bhau took Rs 20 from the wallet and gave only to Arun Ghodke and to none else. Further Bipin Bhau said that this has happened for the first time in many years. Arun considers this as Baba's blessings on him and says emotionally that Baba read his thoughts and fulfilled his desire. He has also shared the picture of the wallet. Picture of the wallet is given below.

Prospects improved after becoming a Baba devotee

Shankar Rajput of Aurangabad became a devotee of Baba in the year 2010. The same year he got married. He had neither a house of his own nor a steady salaried job or a well settled business, though he could make both ends meet. Being married he was quite ambitious to have a house of his own as well as wished to establish a business. Within 6 months he got an offer of a plot in the highway at a reasonable price and he purchased the plot and set up a shop and today his business in tyres is thriving by Baba's grace. He also started construction of his own house. He then went to Shirdi and brought Baba's idol, got it sanctified at Dwarkamai by Baba's touch and installed the same in the shrine of his house. To him everything seemed to be a dream come true as he could never have imagined. "Baba blessed me and made my dreams come true" says Shankar Rajput fully contended.

Anonymous devotee gets job of her dreams

Anonymous devotee says, "we moved to Australia in 2017 because of my husband's job. The initial two years were a period of struggle as I had a difficult time finding a suitable job for myself. I used to keep praying to Baba and read Sri Sai Satcharitra regularly."

"In December 2019, I got a contractual job with a prestigious government department. This was my dream come true job. I had been praying to Baba to get this coveted job since my arrival in Australia."

In June 2020, the devotee says, "the department where I was working went through a complete realignment and my present manager encouraged me to apply for the upcoming permanent roles. Taking Baba's name, I started applying but being a government department, the recruitment process was very slow. Daily I used to read other devotee's experiences on facebook and my faith in Baba kept strengthening. I was interviewed on 10th September which was a Thursday, got my verbal offer on 12th November which was a Thursday and finally got my written offer on 19th November 2020 which again was a Thursday".

Anuradha's offering accepted by Baba

Anuradha of Chennai shares one of her unique experiences. In the year 2016, Anuradha says, "I had the fortune of visiting Shirdi with my friends. I wanted to take some gift to Baba but was unable to decide as to what to take. Seeking Baba's guidance I just opened a page of Sri Sai Satcharitra at random, which happened to be the chapter in which Baba asks Anandrao Phadke to offer a silk bordered dhotar to Shama. I got the hint that Baba wanted me to offer him a dhoti. I purchased an off-white dhoti with a golden border. I decided that after offering the dhoti to Baba, I will give it to someone outside the temple in Shirdi itself.".

While approaching the Samadhi Mandir Anuradha was constantly pleading to Baba to accept her offering. She says, "I had always seen the priests in the temple just touching the "vastra" offerings of the devotees to the Samadhi and returning to the devotees. Most of the time they don't even open the packet. To my surprise, the priest not only opened my packet but unfolded the dhoti and covered the Samadhi of Baba with the dhoti. I couldn't believe my eyes and was full of tears of joy. The priest then returned the dhoti. In a fit of excitement, I hugged the dhoti with tears still rolling down my eyes with devotion, love and gratitude for Baba. For a fraction of a second I decided against gifting the dhoti to anyone in the Mandir premises. I wished to keep it to myself as a blessing from Baba. However, I shooed off my selfish thinking as it would be right on my part to give it to someone who would use it."

"While standing at the prasad counter I saw a person who was standing a little ahead of me dressed like and resembling Baba. However, by the time I collected Udi and came out he was not to be seen anywhere around. Dejected, I went along with my friends to Lendi Bagh and other places. While we were about to leave the place, I saw the same Baba-like person with his back towards me. Immediately I went towards him and requested him humbly to accept the dhoti. He just nodded and accepted it without speaking a word. I thanked him and left the place in a blissful state of mind as I felt that Baba himself had accepted my offering".

"Next morning before leaving Shirdi, I wished to have a quick darshan of Baba. My friends were tired and didn't come. I prayed to Baba to give me a quick darshan as I had to leave Shirdi in one hour. When I went to the entrance, no crowd was there and I reached Baba's Samadhi within a few minutes and had a wonderful darshan of Baba. Neither did I pray nor did I make any special request, I just admired Baba from a distance for about five minutes and left the temple with a sense of gratitude and a peaceful mind. My friends were surprised to see me return so quickly and repented having not accompanied me.

Baba accepts whatever we give with love and faith" says Anuradha with a shine in her eyes and full of devotion to Baba.

Bow to Shri Sai
Peace be to all

CHAPTER 13

BUSINESS / JOB RELATED MATTERS

Letters redirected

Srividhya of New Delhi says once when her husband had issues with his business partner and his business partner was planning to file a case against her husband. In order to prevent him from filing a case, they sent a letter to her husband's business partner stating the facts and that her husband cannot be held responsible for any loss their business was incurring. However, while drafting the letter they had made a minor mistake which gave a contrary meaning to the message and can make her husband accountable in the court of law. When they found out this mistake they were shocked and tried their level best to retrieve the letters sent as registered posts, through the postal department. However, they could not succeed. They sent the letters to the addressee at his home address (old), home address (new) and business address.

They passed about a fortnight or so in extreme anxiety while constantly praying to Baba to rescue them from this situation. Suddenly, one day one of the letters was redirected to them as the house was locked. Letter sent to the new address of the partner also was redirected to them. The letter sent at the business address also was returned as his partner's legal adviser told him not to accept any letter from

Srividhya's husband and also advised him not to proceed with legal action. Srividhya and her family were in disbelief when all their three three letters sent to her husband's business partner returned without being opened by the addressee.

Srividhya with a sigh of relief said that during the period of about a fortnight or so not a single day went without uttering Baba's name. With a cheerful mood she says that it was Baba who had actually protected them from this ticklish situation as it is impossible that all the three letters had been redirected to them without opening.

Baba's endless blessings

Manish of Aurangabad says that he came to Shirdi to visit with his parents after passing his 10th grade exams. He was not very good in his studies and was not sure what he should do to earn his living. His parents enrolled him in Sai Sansthan's ITI and he stayed in Shirdi for two years and completed his course.

With the diploma he acquired, he started working in a small company which closed down after a few years and he became jobless. After this he ventured into a few businesses but that too did not flourish. Finally, he prayed to Baba to help him settle down in life with a steady income which would help him sustain himself and his family. After almost 10 years of unsuccessful and unsteady income, with Baba's blessings, he finally started working as an insurance agent and now he is doing well.

In order to further improve their family's economic condition, his wife also applied for a job as a teacher in a local school. Manish was praying to Baba constantly to help his wife get this job as teacher. There were many hurdles and a stage came where they even lost hope. However, with Baba's grace and blessings, his wife succeeded and is now working as a teacher.

Manish says that he could never believe that he could come up in life to this extent given his poor education background and less qualifications. However, Baba's grace made it possible.

Vennela's patience well rewarded

Vennela of Vijayawada completed her B.Tech in June 2021. While she was studying all her batchmates, juniors and seniors got placements in campus interviews from third year onwards. Even the average and below average students got placements. Only a very few were not selected. Vennela was one of them. Vennela was derided by her relatives and some even spoke sarcastically. Vennela could do nothing but to remain quiet and cool. "Patience is the best gift that I have received from Baba", Venella says. Further, Venella consoles herself saying that "like Shevade in Sai Satcharitra (chapter 48) who was derided for not having been prepared well for his examination, but was confident about his passing the examination as foretold by Baba, she too was confident that Baba will surely bless her with a better job.

In fact, Venella and her family members were very worried and depressed about this as they were at a loss to imagine what would happen after the completion of the course in June 2021. But as usual, Sai Baba came to their rescue. One month before her completion of the course, in the month of May 2021, Venella got a placement with a package far better than her peers and also in a field superior to what she had expected.

With the placement letter in her hand, Venella emotionally said that, "my Baba will never forsake me". All that Baba expects from his devotees is a two paise dakshina of Shraddha and Sabari, which she exhibited in abundance.

Got a job with Baba's grace

Ramya of Hyderabad was working in a private company and was on the lookout for a better job. Despite her best efforts for more than 6 months she couldn't get a job to satisfy her requirements. One of her friends advised her to read Sri Sai Satcharitra and she also told her that Baba will resolve all her worries. As suggested by her friend Ramya started reading Sri Sai Satcharitra and after about four months she got a satisfactory offer in a good company of her choice. In a joyful mood Ramya says "Baba can resolve any major issues, if a devotee sincerely prays to Him".

A competent Dinesh

Dinesh Chandran of Chennai joined a new company recently and due to COVID he had to work from home. Hence he did not get any proper briefing from his superiors as happens in the normal course. One day his boss was on leave and the very same day a very important work was assigned to him. As he did not know how to proceed with the assignment, he prayed to Baba and kept his cool, studied the file carefully and submitted his work. He was neither confident about his output, nor did he consider himself competent to handle the work. He therefore was anxious the whole day.

Next day, to his surprise his seniors had praised him and told him that the work done by him was perfect. Dinesh says, "his faith in Baba alone had made this possible. In fact, it was Baba Who did the work for me".

Got a suitable and an appropriate job with the help of Baba

Sripriya of Chennai says that every night she used to light two lamps in front of Baba's idol praying to get a decent job. She wanted to earn to improve the financial condition of her family and therefore applied for a job in her daughter's school. After sometime the school management called her and asked her if she is willing to take up as a teacher for the first standard. She immediately gave her consent. In three days she got her appointment letter and was also told that she being a teacher of that school her child would get free education, as per the school policy. Hearing this Sripriya says, "I was filled with tears of joy and had no words to thank Baba".

After taking up her assignment as a primary school teacher, she found it very difficult to manage home and office together. She always used to pray to Baba to help. The Baba statue that she had has very big eyes and looking at Baba's eyes she asked Baba, "Are you seeing me? Do you know me?" The same night, she got an answer to her question from Baba in her dream in which Baba told her that "I am always with you looking at you and your welfare".

She says that she couldn't believe that her faith in Baba could do so much wonders to her and change her life totally.

Kiruthika's miracle

Kiruthika of Dubai says that they had entered into a new venture recently and were facing cash flow issues, as any other start-ups do. They had issued post dated cheques (PDC) to their supplier. Their cheques were generally cleared with the payments received from their customers. However, during November 2021, they did not receive the payment from one of their customers. They were worried that their PDC would bounce, if the payment is not received by month end.

It has been their experience that despite rigorous follow up, sometimes payments were not received on time. Suppliers also generally don't agree to present the cheques late. Hesitatingly, and while constantly praying to Baba, they requested the supplier to present the PDC after a week. Surprisingly, he agreed to their request immediately. At the same time they also called the customer asking him to make payment at the earliest. Again she says, the same evening the client also deposited the amount in the bank. Kiruthika says, "Baba not only saved us but also helped us to maintain our company's reputation".

Aishwarya got a job of her choice

Aishwarya was a school topper. She got admission in the college miraculously with Baba's grace. After completion of her higher studies, she prayed to Baba to help her find a stress free job. Aishwarya says happily that "Baba fulfilled that wish also".

She is full of gratitude to Baba and says not a single day she can spend without remembering, praying and seeing Baba.

Bow to Shri Sai
Peace be to all

CHAPTER 14

UDI MIRACLES

Nirmala Mohite rescued by Baba's udi

Nirmala Mohite of Aurangabad had organised an Udyapan ceremony in their house. In that connection all the members of the family went the temple in the morning except Nirmala Mohite who was making all arrangements for the Udyapan ceremony at home. While doing some household work she slipped from the first floor of the house and fell down in the garage, where luckily the car was not there. She fell down from a height of 15 feet on her back and was crying in extreme pain. Hearing the thunderous noise, the neighbours gathered, informed family members and she was rushed to the hospital immediately.

The doctors, after seeing her X-Ray report informed that her spinal cord has broken and a major surgery has to be performed. Further, they said that even after the surgery she will be confined to a wheelchair for a long time. Hearing this all the members of the family were depressed and Sharad, Nirmala's son, could not control his tears and asked Baba as to why this had happened when they were preparing for an Udhyapan ceremony in Baba's honour. After reading Sai Stavana Manjari, Sharad went out to relax his mind. On the way, he met one of his friends and informed him of his mother's condition.

His friend told him not to worry and gave him a packet of Udi which he always carries with him and asked Sharad to apply the same to his mother and also to give her some udi mixed with water to drink. Sharad did as advised by his friend.

The same evening a senior doctor visited the hospital and after seeing the X-Rays and getting preliminary reports from the junior doctors, asked them to take another X-Ray. When the senior doctor saw the second X-Ray he said everything was ok and asked the doctors as to whose X-Ray report they showed him earlier. The junior doctors were astonished to hear this as they were sure that the earlier X-Ray belonged to Nirmala Mohite. On hearing this the whole family was overwhelmed with tears of joy and simply thanked Baba for saving Nirmala Mohite. “It's incredible that a middle aged person falling from 15 feet succumbs only to minor injuries” says Sharad Mohite. She was discharged the same evening. Doctors prescribed a few pain killers. The family distributed the prasad and the other food items prepared for the Udyapan ceremony in the morning to the hospital attendants who were also extremely surprised to hear this miracle. Nirmala Mohite recovered within 3-4 days.

Coma patient comes back to life

Brother-in-law of one of the friend’s of Shankar Rajput of Aurangabad took poison on the Diwali day, i.e., November 4, 2021. He was rushed to the hospital and the doctors told him that he was in coma and the chances of survival are bleak.

After this incident Shankar Rajput went on a ‘pad Yatra’ to Shirdi from Aurangabad with a palki procession and returned on Sunday, November 14, 2021. On return, he enquired from his friend as to how his brother-in-law was. He said that his condition continues to be the same. Immediately he called his friend home and gave him Baba’s Udi and prasad that he brought from Shirdi and told his friend to apply Udi on the forehead of his brother-in-law and keep a little on his mouth as he was being fed using a pipe. His friend did as advised by Shankar and after the application of Udi twice, his brother-in-law gained consciousness, recovered and became well. This is the power of Baba’s Udi. Shankar was at a loss of words in praise of Baba while explaining this to me.

Toothache cured

Anonymous devotee says that she had a severe pain in her tooth and was unable to eat food. She tried a few medicines and since the pain did not abate she decided to visit a dentist. Suddenly a thought arose in her mind to try applying Baba’s udi. She immediately stopped taking all the medicines and started applying udi twice a day on the pain area and wonder of wonders, the pain vanished after 4 applications only. “Such is the power of udi”, says the devotee.

Delivered second child

Jyoti Ankush Ade of Yavatmal, Maharashtra got married in the year 2005 and delivered a baby girl in the year 2006. After that for 10 years she did not conceive. Ashok Jadhav of Aurangabad gave her Baba's Udi and asked her to take Udi with water daily and to chant "Sai, Sai" always. After that she delivered her second child.

Conceived after 12 years

In the year 2017, Ashok Jadhav's distant relative Pushpa from Nashik came and stayed with them. When she reached their house she saw Ashok Jadhav's kids were sitting in the lounge. Looking at the kids she felt like sitting with them and playing with them. She asked them if she could sit and talk with them. Wife of Ashok Jadhav told her not to take permission for such small things. To this, Pushpa said that she was asking permission as no one allows her to play with their kids as she doesn't have a kid and calls her "bhaanj" (infertile).

Hearing this the wife of Ashok Jadhav told her that they don't believe in such things and that it is not her fault. Ashok Jadhav gave her Baba's Udi and asked her to take it regularly and that she will conceive. She looked at him in disbelief. But Ashok Jadhav, in order to instil confidence in her, told her that if you don't conceive, my tongue will be cut. He also added that this is not me, but Baba is saying. She then took some extra Udi from them before leaving. Today, Pushpa is the mother of 8 months' baby.

Abhishek swallowed a box full of udi

Abhishek said when he was in 7th standard, he had malaria and a very high fever. At that time in the local Baba temple some important event was scheduled for which all the members of his family went, leaving him behind. He cried a lot as he could not go to the temple but wanted to go. Suddenly, he went to the shrine in their house, took out the box of udi and swallowed the entire udi in the hope that his fever would go away and he could go to the temple. After five minutes he started sweating profusely and his shivering also stopped. He immediately ran to see his Baba in the temple.

Sai Udi's amazing protection on a devotee's husband

Anonymous devotee says that her husband never consumed any medicines despite the fact that he had diabetes and high blood pressure. He never listened to anyone. Around 15 years back when they went to their family doctor, the doctor threw away his file and refused to treat him as he never consumed medicines. He further said, "I am really surprised to see how with a blood pressure of 250/180 you are coming walking normally to my clinic without any symptoms. I am sure you are really blessed by God".

The devotee, though very much concerned about his condition, was also very happy to hear the words of the doctor because ever since her husband had health issues and knowing his nature of not taking pills, she started using udi, just like salt, in all the food that she cooks. In case her husband is out of station, she used to pray to Baba that I am putting udi in this food, but this udi should reach my husband when he consumes his food. Her husband remained active without any problem till the age of 59+,i.e., 15 years after the above incident.

Crucial decision taken by casting lots before Baba

Sanjay Wagh of Aurangabad says that his daughter was in her 7th month's pregnancy in September 2020. Suddenly, she developed fever, cough, sore throat, etc. all corona like symptoms. He took her to his family doctor who insisted on COVID test. He was very much under mental pressure and was against getting the corona test done especially due to the fear of the consequences including isolation and hospitalisation.

Finally, as per his practice, he cast lots before Baba whether to go for COVID test or not. He received 'NO' as answer from Baba. He felt relieved and with full trust in Baba, he started giving udi mixed with water to her daughter daily. Within 2-3 days the fever started abating and she became alright. In the ninth month, she delivered a healthy baby. All were happy and remained grateful to Baba.

Ramya's miracles

Ramya of Kerala says that in the year 2018-19 there was a small lump in her breast which slowly increased in size day by day. Being very scared, she sat in front of Baba's photo and cried a lot. Then she consumed udi water while praying constantly to Baba to dissolve the lump. Next morning she was surprised to see that her lump had disappeared.

In June 2021, Ramya was blessed with a baby boy. At the time of labour pains she was extremely scared and again consumed udi water while praying to Baba for a safe delivery. Within 15 minutes of the intake of udi water, she delivered without any pain. The doctors and the nurses were very surprised.

Ramya says that Baba was always around her when she called Him. Unaware tears fall from her eyes whenever she utters Baba's name. She says, " I am living because of Baba."

Faith in Baba does wonders

Archana Mohanty of Bhubaneswar says that Baba is not just someone whom she worships but he is more like a family member with whom she shares her happy as well as sad moments. She has firm faith that Baba will protect her and be with her always.

In September 2020, during the pandemic, both Archana and her husband were in home isolation after being tested positive for COVID. It was not possible for them to leave their only young daughter alone and get hospitalised. After a few days, in the evening suddenly Archana's health became extremely serious, pulse rate increased to 140 and oxygen level decreased. Her husband called the doctor who advised immediate hospitalisation, as her condition was serious. Since she could not leave her daughter alone she asked the doctor that she will get hospitalised next morning. However, the doctor insisted on immediate hospitalisation.

Again while constantly praying to Baba she requested her doctor who then agreed to her request. She kept praying to Baba non-stop till she slept. Her husband also gave her udi water from time to time. At night she saw Baba in my dream sitting beside her and telling "why worry when I'm with you ". After this dream she suddenly woke up but could continue to feel the presence of Baba with her. Seeing her awake, her husband checked her pulse rate which was normal and oxygen level had also increased. Soon she felt relieved and her worries disappeared.

Diabetes cured miraculously

Rajeswari of Vijayawada says that about a year back she was diagnosed with diabetes. Hearing this she became excessively tense as she is scared of diabetes. Because of this excessive tension, she got BP and vertigo. All her family members started scolding her that for the fear of one disease she has invited two more.

In the meantime, she also got gastritis due to which she could not eat anything. Her condition seemed very bad and her daily routine got affected.

At this time, keeping aside her fear, being an ardent devotee of Baba, she started taking udi with everything that she consumed including with medicines, while praying to Baba to cure her of all her ailments.

During her follow up visit, her doctor was surprised to see that her BP and sugar were normal. Her vertigo and gastritis also did not recur. Rajeshwari, while expressing her gratitude to Baba with a smiling face says "Baba has cured me completely with His udi".

Bow to Shri Sai
Peace be to all

CHAPTER-15

MAJESTIC MIRACLES

Why fear when Baba, Baba, everywhere

In the year 2013 on a Thursday around 4 a.m, Radhakrishnan of New Delhi saw an extremely bright light in his bedroom. He got up to check if, by mistake, the lights remained on in any of the rooms. He found that all the rooms were dark except in the shrine where a zero watt bulb was glowing as usual. But the light in his bedroom continued to be there and he came back and lied down facing the ceiling. Suddenly, the light started decreasing in size gradually and started revolving at the centre of his forehead in a very small size like that of a "bindi" for a long time which he could not look at given its high speed. Later on, suddenly, he felt that the light went inside his body. After sometime he started feeling uneasy. He therefore got up, refreshed himself and came back and tried to sleep again. The restlessness in his body continued for about half an hour and then he fell asleep.

Radhakrishnan consulted one of his Gurus whom he follows reverentially and explained the above incident to him and asked him about its significance. His Guruji explained to him that Baba had shown him Kakad Aarti. He further said, "Baba doesn't want to leave you but be with you as He is very happy with your constant Annadaan and other noble services and hence the light entered you". Readers can imagine what would have been the plight of Radhakrishnan at that time.

As mentioned by his Guruji, Radhakrishnan says he could feel the presence of Baba always, everywhere within him and outside. If travelling by public transport, the vehicle would have Baba's picture, if he was driving and stopped at signals, the vehicle in front would have Baba's photo on the back window, and so on. He says he always have a GPS, i.e., Guru Positioning System in his life which guides him in the right direction.

Bharati's backache cured

Bharati from Bengaluru suffered in the year 2010 from a severe back ache and was not even able to move. Even with the treatments and physiotherapy her condition did not improve except that she was able to walk a little bit in January 2011 but could not bend down, sit, etc.

Given her health condition she resigned from her job and went to stay with her daughter who was studying MBBS in Mandya. Most of the time she was confined to bed and walking only for very essential day to day needs. All that she could do was to stand or lie down. Getting up from the bed was the most difficult task.

Bharati had the regular habit of reading Sri Sai Satcharitra, which she continued lying in the bed and often looking at Baba's picture on the wall. One Thursday, she had requested one of her neighbour's to buy bananas to offer as prasad for Sai Baba. She kept the bananas (around half a dozen) on the table near the shrine. Just near the shrine was a glass sliding door leading to the balcony where her maid was drying clothes. After finishing her work she left the sliding door open.

Bharati prayed to Baba and asked Him as to when He will cure her and make her functional, and went for an afternoon nap. Suddenly, her sleep was disturbed as the neighbours were calling her loudly and were saying that a monkey had entered her house and taken away the bananas. Hearing this, with great difficulty she managed to go to the balcony only to see the monkey sitting on top of the 2nd floor terrace of her neighbour. It was looking at her. Immediately she came in and locked the door.

Bharati, standing in front of Sai Baba's picture on the wall, looked at Him and cryingly said "Sai, today no prasad for You and me. I will stay hungry today. How can I again find someone to buy fruits when I can't even walk to go to the shop! You are really making me feel helpless. So much of unbearable pain. I don't have any hope. Just have to live for my daughter's sake. Why don't You understand my plight? I want the bananas back from the monkey and I want You to cure me Sai." After her conversation with Baba she went and lied down.

Suddenly she heard a continuous tap on the glass door of her balcony and her neighbours shouting at her, "aunty the monkey is at your balcony". Hearing this with great struggle she went near the balcony and saw that the monkey was tapping the glass door standing on the balcony. The monkey was standing with the banana bunch and tears rolling down its eyes. The monkey was tapping on the door and crying.

Bharati opened the door, bent down and took the bananas thanking the monkey for returning the same for offering to Baba. She closed the door and had a bath and performed her Thursday's Pooja and Aarti for Sai Baba. She noticed the monkey was still sitting on the balcony whimpering. She gave 2 bananas to the monkey with a sense of gratitude.

Then she started preparing lunch for her daughter. When she returned, she narrated that day's incident to her daughter, who after listening, exclaimed, " Ma! You are sitting down. Sai has cured you!!".

Bharati says with tears welled up in her eyes that "I realised only then that I had bent down to pick the fruits from the balcony and sat on a small stool in the pooja room to read 108 Sai namavali and performed Baba's aarti bending forward". She couldn't control her tears of joy and said feelingly

“SAI HAS CURED ME’. With a grateful shine on her eyes she said, “Why fear when our Sai is always here”.
Bharti’s neighbours told her that the monkeys had never returned anything that they took away. This is the first time that they have returned. “This is nothing but a Sai miracle”, the neighbours admitted.

Padmini getting indications of future events in the form of dream

Padmini Jayaraman of Coimbatore says that her life is full of miracles. She gets vision of future incidents in dream, though she would never know the significance of the dream at that time. Once she saw in her dream that she and her husband were going in a chauffeur driven car in a desert area. She informed her husband about this dream.

After a few years her husband got a good offer of appointment in Saudi Arabia and he moved to Jeddah. Later when Padmini joined him after he settled down there, while entering the house she had goosebumps as she saw the same house in her dream sometime back. True to her dream, her husband was provided with a chauffeur driven car.

Padmini, even after many years of their marriage, didn’t have a child. One day in her dream, in the same house in Jeddah, she saw a person clad in a saffron coloured cloth giving her two babies wrapped in a green coloured cloth. She told this to her

husband and her husband also could not make out whom Padmini saw in her dream based on her description.
Later when they returned to India, in the year 2004, her sister asked Padmini to accompany her to Shirdi. Padmini refused. At that time she didn't know who Sai Baba was. Again after a month or so when her sister asked her to accompany her to Shirdi, she accepted, but didn't know why. After reaching Shirdi the next day, Padmini's sister asked her to get up around 2:30 in the morning to go to the temple for Kakad Aarti. Padmini, who was still in a drowsy state, told her that she doesn't want to come at that hour but will visit the temple the next day. On her sister's insistence she agreed unwillingly.

When they were standing in the queue at the temple Padmini, being annoyed with her sister for waking her up so early, stood little far away from her sister. Her sister repeatedly asked her to come next to her. She told her that it doesn't make any difference if she stands next to her or a few feet away. Her sister had to keep quiet to avoid unnecessary arguments.

When they reached the Samadhi Mandir entrance, her sister went inside and a few others behind her followed her. When Padmini was about to enter, the security guard closed the gate. Despite her sister requesting the security guard to allow Padmini, being her sister, the security guard refused and told her in Hindi "aap kal aayiye" (you come tomorrow). At that time Padmini felt that she was being slapped and that was the turning point in her life.

Next morning to the surprise of all, Padmini woke up early and went alone to the temple and had a darshan of Sai Baba. On seeing the beautiful statue of Baba in the temple, she at once recollected that it was Baba Who had come in her dream when she was in Jeddah and gave her two babies clad in green cloth.

In Shirdi, Padmini lost her handbag containing her gold chain, earrings and some cash. While she was feeling bad for the loss of her handbag, somebody told her that it is a good omen to lose money, valuables, etc. in a holy place, as it is tantamount to washing away our sins.

Again, before leaving Shirdi when they all went to the temple, her sister told the priest that Padmini doesn't have a kid and asked them to bless her. He gave a coconut and told Padmini and her husband to eat it in the form of a sweet. Padmini did as advised.

During the same year her husband had consulted some astrologer regarding the prospects of an issue for them. To this he answered in a quizzical way in Tamil *"Attoram pen deivam, mamanar poorvigam".* In English it translates something similar to "*Riverside Goddess; Father in law's native*". They couldn't understand anything.

Later one day, Padmini attended a Sai Baba Bhajan in her friend's house. The lady of the house was a very very staunch devotee of Baba and it is said that she can listen to Baba speak to her and conveys to others the reply Baba gives. When Padmini went and consulted her, she said Baba is asking her to visit their Family God's temple, Perur Angalamman.

At that time she came to know that no one in her family ever worshipped their family's Deity for as long as 100 years and hence they were having troubled lives. Having come to know about who their family Goddess was, Padmini, her husband and her mother-in-law went to Perur to visit their Family Goddess temple. When they reached their destination, no one knew about this temple. They searched for a long time and lost hope. Her husband was about to return when Padmini insisted on making one last attempt.

She went to the nearby shop and asked if they knew where Perur Angalamman temple was. At this very moment one lady in red saree, with a bright red bindi, held her hand and said, "I know, come I will take you there". She accompanied them in their car and dropped them in front of the temple. When they got down and about to enter the temple, they wanted to thank the lady and turned but found no one there, despite searching for her everywhere. They visited their Family Deity on February 5, 2005. On March 5, 2005, she conceived and delivered twins on October 23, 2005, after 14 years of their marriage.

When her twins were growing, Padmini says they used to stare at Baba's image even as a small baby of 4-5 months. The first letter that her kids uttered was "Baba" unlike other kids uttering mama, papa, tata, etc.

Padmini says reverentially that Baba has changed her life totally and now every breath she takes is because of Baba. Padmini wondered how Baba had hinted her regarding twins in her dream; arranged her visit to Shirdi; made her lose her ornaments and thus washed away her sins; made her visit her Family Goddess who was not worshipped for more than 100 years; etc. and says "everything seems to be a miracle".

Further, recently, a year and a half back an old, around 90 years, visited her house enquiring about some address in that area. He sat in the portico and Padmini offered him water. When she told him no such address is there in that area, he left. She has been residing in that area for more than 20-25 years and she knows every nook and corner of that area. She said that the address that he was looking for was not there at all. On the same evening, when she went near one of the trees in her house where she regularly lights a lamp, she saw a vague image of a deity on the tree. The picture of the tree is given below.

Immediately she called her Guru whom she regards high, and asked him of its significance. He told her that the image is of Baba and that Baba resides in their house. Hearing this, in hindsight, she came to the conclusion that the old man who visited her house is none other than Baba as he was asking for an address which never existed.

Bow to Shri Sai
Peace be to all

CHAPTER 16

LEGAL AND PROPERTY RELATED ISSUES

Timely assistance by Baba

Rajeswari of Vijayawada says that her husband, Seshu Kumar, was a sincere and obedient son to his parents. He serves them without any expectations. While this quality is very good, the very same quality had been used by his brothers to their advantage; his parents too, according to her, did not recognise the real and selfless service of her husband and incline more towards her husband's brothers. The other brothers took away her husband's share of property and business and her husband never questioned them.

Despite all this, Rajeswari is content with what they have and remains grateful to Baba for keeping them secure. Once her husband's elder brother wanted Rs.18 lakhs and borrowed the same from a broker out of which Rs. 9 lakhs was paid by her husband and Rs. 9 lakhs by her brother-in-law. When the amount was not paid on time, the money lender filed a case against both her husband and brother-in-law. Her brother-in-law, being an influential person, got rid of the legal proceedings. Her husband continued to remain embroiled in this mess.

One day, to their surprise, the tenant in her mother-in-law's residence, of their own accord, came forward to help them. They engaged a renowned lawyer, who won the case in their favour. The court ordered Seshu Kumar to pay the remaining amount without any interest, which was a great relief for them. Rajeswari says "when a devotee totally surrenders to Baba, Baba himself takes care of the devotees' needs."

Job related legal issues

Jayaraman was working in Gokulam Chit Funds. He applied for leave for his daughter's medical treatment, which the company refused. However, he returned to his native place after giving a proper leave application. In the meantime, the company charged him with false allegations and filed a case in the court. The matter went to the court of law and was tried several times. His case moved from lower court to High Court and ultimately to Supreme Court. In all the trials he was provided with a free public prosecutor and he argued very effectively and finally the ordered Gokulam Chit Funds to reinstate Jayaraman with full salary and other perks along with arrears from the day he proceeded on leave.

Jayaraman says, it was Baba who became Judge in all the cases for him. He further adds that ever since he became a devotee of Sai Baba, his prospects improved. He is at a loss of words to thank Baba who has provided him with every comfort in his life.

Change in brother's attitude

Jayaraman's father was critically ill and hospitalised. He visited his father and applied Baba's udi to his forehead and chest. Surprisingly, his father was alright the next morning and had tea/coffee and snacks. Since his condition had improved considerably, he was discharged the same day. Jayaraman also returned to Calicut.

Within a month, he received a message that his father passed away. After performing the final rites of his father, his younger brother who had always been manipulating his father's property, handed over to him a copy of the document giving details of his father's property / money etc. duly signed by him and a witness. He was surprised to see the sudden changed attitude of his brother.

He just can't remain without saying that, it is Baba's miracle that has worked in his life.

Bow to Shri Sai
Peace be to all

CHAPTER-17

TIMELY RESCUE

Nageshwara Rao saved from huge loss

Nageshwara Rao, once collected an amount of Rs. 5,00,000 on behalf of the company and went to deposit the amount with the company Accountant. At that time, he received a call from his wife saying that their son was suffering from constant high fever and that he should return home urgently. In a hurry he left without taking a receipt for the amount of Rs. 5,00,000 paid to the Accountant. Next day the Accountant denied having received any money from Nageshwara Rao. Nageshwara Rao was in a fix and in the absence of any proof he could do nothing but to keep quiet. For Nageshwara Rao repaying Rs. 5 lakhs may take a long period of time. In the meantime, the Accountant furnished her house, by spending a huge amount. It became evident to Nageshwara Rao that she had used his money. However, without proof Nageshwara Rao couldn't do anything.

He and his wife kept praying in front of Baba's photo the whole night. Next morning when Nageshwara Rao went to office, the Accountant on her own came and returned Rs. 2.5 lakhs and apologised. She also said that she has already spent Rs. 2.5 lakhs and cannot refund the same.

When the matter became public in the office, given the wonderful track record of Nageshwara Rao, his office colleagues together pooled Rs. 1.5 lakhs in order to help him come out of this financial mess. He had to pay Rs. 1 lakh from his pocket. Though the matter ended here, Nageshwara Rao got a lifetime lesson to be vigilant while dealing with monetary matters.

Saved from accident

Dinesh Chandran of Chennai says that it is his habit that he always thinks about something or the other even while driving. His mind never remains calm without thinking. One day while he was returning home on his bike he was so engrossed in his thoughts that he did not see a huge truck coming in the opposite direction very close to his bike. When he saw the truck suddenly, he was sure that the accident was inevitable. But even before he could think of anything, he saw the truck crossing with only a hairline distance and went away. For a minute, he says, “I was panic struck and couldn’t believe that nothing happened to me and I was safe”. At this time away he saw Sai Baba's picture in the key chain of his bike and understood the permanent protective shield of Baba, as otherwise it is impossible that a huge truck comes so close and still he remains unhurt.

Ramanjaneyulu in safe hands

Ramanjaneyulu of Hyderabad, a staunch devotee of Baba, was travelling by a bike 2-3 days before his marriage when he met with an accident and lost consciousness. He was wearing a gold chain, ring, etc. and was carrying Rs. 30,000 cash. A passer by in saffron coloured clothes saw Ramanjaneyulu in an unconscious state. He immediately took out his gold chain, ring and the cash that he had, kept them in a saffron coloured cloth and tied them securely before rushing him to the hospital. On the way to the hospital, the man in saffron coloured clothes tried calling all the people in the telephone list with a view to informing his relatives. Hearing this, his relatives reached the hospital. The man in saffron coloured clothes handed over Ramanjaneyulu's personal belongings to his relatives. Given the emergency situation all were in a tense mood and did not even thank him for his help in providing Ramanjaneyulu timely medical assistance and keeping his belongings safe. Suddenly, in a minute or two having come to senses when they searched for the well wisher who brought Ramanjaneyulu to the hospital he was not found despite their best efforts.

They all, being a staunch devotee of Baba, concluded that it was Baba who had rescued Ramanjaneyulu on time. With the timely medical care received, Ramanjaneyulu gained consciousness and was discharged the same night and his wedding which was scheduled to take place in two three days time also went off very well.

Hernia Surgery Averted

Sirisha from Texas says recently her father suffered from umbilical hernia. The doctor suggested surgery. The family took it to be a simple surgery but they came to know through doctors that even hernia surgery could be risky if there be any complication in the heart. Her father, being a heart patient, the family was scared to go for the surgery. Sirisha kept praying to Baba all the time to cure her father without a surgery.

Then they consulted their family doctor. He said that hernia size is very small and hence it could be healed with hernia binder. They followed the advice of the family doctor and now Sirisha's father is completely normal with the binder. Sirisha thanked Baba for averting her father's surgery.

Hit by a granite slab

In September 2020, a granite slab which was becoming loose due to heavy rains and constant seepage, fell off in Shyamala's head. She was hurt at the centre and three sides of her head and was bleeding profusely. She was rushed to the hospital. They had difficulty in finding a good doctor due to COVID.

When her injuries were cleaned the doctors and others were surprised to see that she had only minor cuts on the skin and there were no deep injuries in the skull. Shyamala emotionally says that it was Baba who saved her by keeping His hand over her head because after such a huge and heavy granite slab falling on the head, anyone will go into coma. Shyamala remains thankful to Baba for rescuing her from the serious effects on her wounds.

After one year of this incident, she went to her heart specialist for her angio review. The heart specialist was aware of the above incident, and asked Shyamala in astonishment, "you are alive without any complications?" And after seeing her latest angio reports told her "now you don't come to hospital for another 4-5 years. Keep your BP and sugar under control".

Fresh lease of life given by Baba to Vinesh Gokul Jadhav

Ashok Baliram Jadhav of Aurangabad says that his nephew Vinesh Gokul Jadhav was waiting on the platform for his train when a speeding Chennai Express train passed through Shivaji Nagar station while Vinesh was waiting on the platform for his train. Suddenly he fell down unconscious. No one knows whether the speeding train hit him or he got a shock because of the speeding train. But he fell unconscious. The police authorities checked and confirmed that Vinesh was dead and covered his body with a shroud. A 70 year old man who was present there removed the shroud of Vinesh Gokul Jadhav and checked his pulse and said that he is alive. The police authorities insisted that he was dead. To this the 70 year old man told them that if he is not taken to the hospital immediately he will file a case against them. The police then checked and were shocked to see him pulsating and immediately admitted him to Sassoon hospital in Pune. One of the doctors (orthopaedist) in Sassoon hospital was a relative of Ashok Jadhav and recognising Vinesh Gokul Jadhav, he immediately informed Ashok Jadhav about the critical condition of Vinesh and also informed that the chances of survival are very less, as he was already 99.99% dead. Ashok Jadhav told them to start the treatment forthwith. The boy was in a coma and the treatment commenced. After 26 days Vinesh gained consciousness. Vinesh also recognised his relative Rahul Prakash Jadhav and conversed in sign language. Within 5 days, i.e., on the 31st day he had 80% improvement in his condition. Doctors warned the family to refrain from reminding past incidents that may take him to coma again.

On the 36th day he was discharged and taken to his village Darati. After a month when Ashok Jadhav enquired from Vinesh about his condition, Vinesh told that he was fine. Ashok Jadhav asked him as to how the accident occurred. Vinesh told him that he knew nothing about the accident except that he was repeatedly listening to Baba's Aarti using headphones.

His coming back to life hale and hearty and the old man lifting his shroud and insisting that he is alive all seems to be a miracle and all were convinced that the old man was none other than Baba himself. How could Baba not take care of a devotee who was mesmerised in Him!

After this incident, the whole family became a Sai devotee.

Sai Saved the life of Swarna Latha

In May 2012, Murali Krishna from Hyderabad and his family, consisting of his wife and two kids, went for an outing with his office colleagues during a weekend. They went to Shivpuri in the Shivalik ranges about 50 kilometers above Rishikesh. The following day, they decided to go for white water rafting on the river Ganga - an extremely dangerous and challenging outdoor recreational activity. This is ventured out along with a professional raft guide and the rafters are fully equipped.

One raft had 8 person capacity with a trained professional guide. The Guide briefed them about the difficulties and risks that might arise while rafting, DOs and DON'Ts, safety precautions, etc.
All were excited about their first rafting adventure and enjoyed playing with the river water sprinkling on

co-rafters. The guide, from time to time, warned them about the difficulties and risks that they may face through the rocky narrow paths through which the river flows very fast creating big tides which have the capacity to turn the raft upside down. Hence perfect coordination among rafters is essential to sail smoothly through rapids. Knowledge of swimming is essential for Grade IV rapid and above.

Soon they reached a grade III rapid. With less difficulty and more excitement, they sailed through the rapid. As they approached Grade IV - Roller Coaster - they saw a huge tide rising and lifting the raft from the front left corner and within a fraction of a second the raft got lifted high and turned upside down. Murali Krishna says, "I was thrown into the water and was struggling under the water. With great difficulty I came out and got hold of the raft. The life jacket helped me float on the water. Then I realized that except the guide and two others all the rest fell into the water and one by one started surfacing. Within a few seconds all the rafters returned except my wife, Swarna Latha. While I was anxiously looking for her, after about 15 to 20 seconds, she came out of the water just beside the raft struggling hard to breathe. Immediately the guide pulled her into the raft. She continued to gasp. Seeing her back in the raft I had a sigh of relief".

Once Swarna Latha gained strength, she said she was trapped under the raft and had difficulty in pushing it either side to help herself come out. Not knowing how to swim, she was struggling. For a moment she thought that it was the last few minutes of her life. At this moment, she prayed to Baba and said, "You are the only Saviour now". Just then, a hand got hold of her right hand and pulled her up from inside the water. Soon she touched the top edge of the raft and was taken inside by the guide. Swarna Latha said to her husband, "if you had not extended your hand, I would have drowned." Hearing this Murali Krishna surprisingly told her, "how could I extend any help to you when I myself was struggling.". Others also confirmed that they never helped anyone as they were themselves trying to get into the raft. It was at that moment Swarna Latha realised that hearing her prayers, Baba came to her rescue. Swarna Latha feels truly blessed to have sensed Baba's divine touch.

Sai Baba says in Sri Sai Satcharitra Chapter 3, that "**I shall draw out devotees from the jaws of death**". The stories of Vinesh Jadhav and Swarna Latha are a typical manifestation of the above dictum of Baba.

Bow to Shri Sai
Peace be to all

CHAPTER 18

WEDDING DAY BLESSINGS

Baba attending Shyamala's marriage

Shyamala Kasthuri of Hyderabad came to know about Baba after her engagement. She received Sri Sai Satcharitra from one of her friends. She immediately completed reading the book. One story that she liked was "Baba visiting Hemadpant's house in the form of His picture" and also Baba's assurance, "my bones will speak to you".

She therefore decided to test Baba. She told Baba, "I am not your devotee; I don't know who You are; I have no feeling for you; but if you really run to your devotees when they call, I want to see if You are coming for my marriage".

On the day of the marriage, they were getting ready for Gouri Pooja during Brahma Muhurtham. Around 4 a.m. her father's very close classmate came from Chennai to Hyderabad and gave her a long tube-like gift. When she opened it, she saw a beautiful 3 feet size image of Sai Baba. At the bottom of the picture was written **"I will not let anyone down who believes me"** Looking at the picture and the words, tears started rolling down her eyes and all were asking her as to why she was crying. When she told them about the reason all were wonderstruck. Then Baba's image was placed in the central area of the wedding hall and it seemed as if Baba himself was conducting the marriage, Shyamala said.

Baba blessing Purnima Ramani on her wedding day

Sharada Ramani of Coimbatore shares her unforgettable story. Sharada and her husband saw a picture of Baba in the marriage photographs of a Sai devotee. "Baba was not visible during the event, however he was clearly visible in the photographs", says Sharada. On seeing this miracle, her husband immediately prayed to Baba to bless their daughter's wedding with His presence. The wedding took place in Chennai in November 2015.

The year 2015 witnessed Chennai's worst ever floods. On the day of the marriage, November 13, 2015, it was raining heavily and the beautician reached the venue around 5:40 a.m. While she was dressing up the bride, Sharada's husband walked in and said, "I don't see Baba, he has not come". Hearing this the beautician immediately asked, "you mean Shirdi Sai Baba?'. On his saying "Yes", she immediately showed her ring which had Baba's picture with a folded leg covering her entire ring finger. Even before we could say anything she said Baba is dressing up your daughter for the wedding.
The beautician further added that due to rains she could not take out her car from the garage which was flooded with water nor did her driver come. All the taxi/auto/cab she called refused to come to that area

due to heavy flooding. Suddenly she saw an auto and the auto driver also agreed to drop her at the wedding hall where she was bound to. As she was about to sit in the auto she saw OM SAI RAM written in the auto. She being a staunch devotee of Baba thought that Baba came to her rescue. The auto driver drove through the flooded roads with ease and dropped her at the right time. He charged her only the meter amount, which is unheard of in Chennai.

Sharada says, "we were utterly dumbfounded to hear this from her as my brother-in-law, who is also living in the same area where the beautician lives, called an hour ago regretting his inability to attend the marriage as his car was almost drowned in water and no cabs were operating in that area".

Seeing this miracle of Baba, their faith in Baba intensified. Sharada says "not only did Baba accept the invitation of my husband, but also ensured that the marriage takes place smoothly and successfully".

Bow to Shri Sai
Peace be to all

CHAPTER 19

LOST AND FOUND

Lost money retrieved in a strange manner

Abhishek from Vijayawada says that he belongs to a very poor family and his mother saves money with great difficulty and tries to secure the savings in safe investment. Once she had saved around Rs. 30,000 and wrapped it safely in a cover for depositing. When she went to take the money, it was not found. His father generally has the habit of taking money without asking and hence they thought that he had taken it. However, when they checked with him and he denied having taken any money. They made a thorough search but couldn't find the packet with money.

Next day, suddenly a dog entered their house and Abhishek gave the dog some rice and curd to eat and the dog ate it and went away. Abhishek too went outside to close the door. When he reached the main door to close it, suddenly he noticed something floating in the sewer outside his house. He picked up the packet that was floating with the help of a stick and found that it had Rs. 30,000 in it. He felt very happy that his mother's hard earned money had been retrieved. He said it was Baba who came to their house in the form of a dog and helped him find the lost money.

Gayathri found her lost jewels

Gayathri of Hyderabad faces a lot of criticism from her in-laws and remains under constant pressure at her home front. Once while taking her jewels to wear for a function, she was shocked to see the jewels missing. Then constantly praying to Baba, again after a few minutes, she started searching at the same place where she kept her jewels. Strange to say that the jewels which were missing five minutes ago and could not be found despite a thorough search were seen in the same place where she kept them. She was in tears of joy and full of gratitude to Baba, because she knows if the jewels were not found, her in-laws would blow the issue out of proportion to the extent of her losing mental peace.

Lost ring found

Dinesh Chandran of Chennai says that on October 6, 2021 night, being very tired, he dozed off early unaware. Next morning when he woke up his gold ring was missing. He and his mother searched everywhere at home but couldn't find it. He searched everywhere from his office cab to cabin, but could not find the ring. While in office, he kept praying to Baba to help him find the ring as the ring had an emotional value for him since he purchased the gold ring from his first salary.

The same evening, i.e., October 7, 2021, after reaching home he started searching for the ring while constantly repeating Baba's name. Surprisingly within a minute he found the ring whereas during his thorough search in the morning he couldn't find it. This is the power of two letters "BABA".

Lost Sri Sai Satcharitra book returned to Rani Ravi

Rani Ravi from Chidambaram says in the 1990s while she was working in an aided school her senior officer's grandson was hopsitalised. They were very much depressed. Sympathising with his daughter's condition, she being a devotee of Baba, gave her senior officer's daughter her only copy of Sri Sai Satcharitra to be kept near the boy while consoling her that Baba will cure her son. During those days it was not easy to find Sri Sai Satcharitra book. She got the book with great efforts and used to read regularly.

By Baba's grace the child recovered after the surgery. Once the boy was discharged, she requested the boy's mother to return her book. To her surprise she was told that the book was misplaced and could not be found. With a view not to have any ill feelings with her boss and his family, she kept quiet, though she felt dejected and did not relish food. She strongly believed that the boy got well at that time only because of the book. After 10 years, the boy passed away due to multiple disorders.

Few days passed after this incident. One day, a few guests came to her house and by mistake one of the guests left behind Sri Sai Satcharitra. On top of the book were the prasad of vermilion, turmeric, sandal paste, vibhuti, etc. Immediately she informed one of the group members and they contacted the owner of the book. Next the day the owner of the book called her and asked her to keep the book for her use. She thanked Baba for returning the book with His blessings. She lost the Tamil version of the book, but received the English version. Rani happily says that the book helped in improving her English language.

Lost property documents retrieved

Rajeswari of Vijayawada says her parents, who stayed in Pune, used to frequently visit them in Vijayawada, as her father, Sivarama Rao, was in the real estate business in Vijayawada and had rented out his house in Vijayawada. Her father is a very active, organised and a disciplined person. After his retirement from Government service he started his real estate business and handled the business alone very meticulously without any help.

Once when her parents were staying in Rajeswari's house her father misplaced his property document. The value of that property was around Rs. 3 crores.

Hearing this her mother casually remarked that her father had never in his life misplaced a single document, but for the first time while being in Rajeswari's house he lost it. Rajeswari felt very much pained by this casual remark of her mother and prayed to Baba to help her father retrieve the document at the earliest. Her parents were very religious but never believed in Baba, whereas Rajeswari was a very staunch devotee of Baba right from her childhood. When Rajeswari prayed to Baba, her parents asked her as to "what will Your Baba do?". She replied that she believes in Baba and He will help in getting back the documents.

Having misplaced the documents Rajeshwari's father Sivarama Rao decided to go to his own house thinking that if anyone finds the papers, will return to the address as given in the property documents. Without disturbing the tenants, he sat in the Security Guard's room. After a few hours of waiting, three gentlemen came on a bike and stopped in front of the house. Sivarama Rao was extremely happy to see that the three young boys came with his misplaced documents. In appreciation of their kind gesture, Sivarama Rao gave them Rs. 2000.

When he narrated this to his family, Rajeswari thanked Baba for his timely assistance and told her parents happily that Sai Baba heard her prayers. Lord Dattatreya is a syncretic deity considered to be an incarnation of Lord Brahma, Vishnu and Shiva. She considered the three youths in the bike as Lord

Dattatreya. Sai Baba is regarded as the embodied form of Lord Dattatreya. The amount of Rs. 2000 that her father gave to the three persons is the Dakshina that he had paid to Dattatreya.

This incident changed the views of her parents regarding Sai Baba and her father immediately prayed to Baba that if his pending property issues get resolved, he would visit Shirdi. Needless to say, his prayer was fulfilled and he went to Shirdi.

Rajeswari, an ardent devotee of Baba, felt very happy that her parents also have started believing in Baba.

Bow to Shri Sai
Peace be to all

CHAPTER 20

BABA'S PROTECTIVE UMBRELLA

Invisible protection of Baba

Once Srividhya of New Delhi, along with her husband and 2 year old son went out for a walk when they came across a temple where there was a huge crowd to have darshan of a great saint who had visited the temple. Srividhya generally doesn't have the habit of going to the temples and she was about to pass by the temple when her son suddenly started running towards the temple. In order to bring their son back both Srividhya and her husband followed their son but since her son was running fast before she could stop him, her son stood in front of the saint. Seeing her, the saint immediately got up with folded hands and said, "Baba". Being confused she looked behind but no one was there. Then the saint told her that she doesn't need anybody's protection as Baba is behind her.

Srividhya then realised that she had the blessings and protective shield of Baba always along with her which had been extricating her and her family safely and securely from the tough situations in their life. She felt very happy,.

Baba's picture in tact, despite heavy winds

One afternoon, Rani Ravi of Chidambaram, after finishing her household work, was lying down to relax as she had pain in her legs. All of a sudden heavy winds started blowing. She was scared that the Baba's picture kept in the window might fall. While she was trying to get up, she heard the sound of a photo falling down. Filled with fear she went to the next room where she saw Baba's picture resting securely in one of the containers kept below the window. There was no damage to the picture.

Idol's Neck broken

Lalitha of Bengaluru, went for routine medical tests in August 2021. It has always been her practice to carry a small Baba's idol with her whenever she goes to her doctor. She had undergone various blood tests and scans. After all the tests finished the doctor told her that everything was normal. When she returned home she removed the idol from her handbag to put it back in the shrine. To her surprise the idol's neck was broken and she felt depressed..

The very next day she was reading an article on Baba in which one of the devotees mentioned that her Baba idol's neck was broken and what does it signify. It was mentioned that whenever we go through health issues Baba suffers on our behalf and hence the breaking of the neck is to be taken as a good omen as it denotes that we are under Baba's protective umbrella. Reading this article she felt that Baba himself gave her a reply to calm her stressed mind.

Incredible experience of Abhishek

Abhishek from Vijayawada went for a training course in Mumbai in 2016. He was very nervous as that was the first time that he was going to Mumbai and also the first time by flight. He constantly prayed to Baba to help him meet some known person with whom he could be comfortable in the flight.

In the flight, his next seat passenger was an elderly person. After a while he - whom Abhishek refers to as uncle - started talking to Abhishek in Telugu and Abhishek felt comfortable with him. On reaching Mumbai, his uncle helped him in getting a cab for the place of his training. Almost when he was about to reach the destination, he received a message from the organisers of training that the training venue had changed. He found out that the new venue was around 40 kms away from the old venue.

At around 10 p.m. Abhishek called the organisers and requested them to help him reach the new venue. However, being very late, he was asked to reach the new venue on his own and that they will take care of the rest. As it was very late Abhishek, to be safe, decided to spend a night in a lodge and proceed the next morning to the new venue. He tried to get some accommodation. However, since the room rent was Rs. 3000, he decided to spend the night on the road and proceed early in the morning. At this very moment he got a call from his uncle enquiring about his safe arrival. When he explained everything to him, he immediately reached the spot where Abhishek was and took him to his hotel room and offered him bread and jam to eat. Thanking his uncle, he went to sleep.

Next morning around 3:30 am, his uncle woke him up and asked him to get ready. He booked a cab and gave him Rs. 100 for breakfast and bade him goodbye. He was really pleased to see that despite being a stranger he was a very helpful person. Once Abhishek reached his destination he tried to call his uncle to inform him of his safe arrival. When he called he found that the number didn't exist.

Abhishek was astonished and he could sense very well that his uncle was none other than Sai Baba himself.

Bow to Shri Sai
Peace be to all

CHAPTER 21

GRACED BY BABA'S DARSHAN

How Jyoti was blessed by Baba

Jyoti of Bengaluru says, "I had the good fortune of visiting Shirdi regularly for the past 8 years with a friend of mine. In 2019 February, much as I had desired, I couldn't join my friend as my daughter had her internal exams".

Jyothi not only felt sad for missing the opportunity to visit Shirdi, but remained obsessed with this thought for a long time. In the month of October 2019, one day while she was scrolling through her messages in the social media she came across a message which said, "I know you are unhappy that you couldn't visit Shirdi. See how surprisingly I will bring you to Shirdi". She was stunned to see this message and was constantly thinking how Baba would execute it. Next morning the same friend asked her if she would visit Shirdi with her.

While preparing for her trip, she came across a bundle of 50 and 10 rupee notes which she had reserved several years ago for distribution to poor and needy and had completely forgotten. She took those currency notes and distributed the money to the poor and needy on her first day of arrival in Shirdi. Only a very few were remaining.

A day before her departure from Shirdi, she was sitting in the temple premises when an old man dressed like Baba approached her and asked for alms. She gave a 50 rupee note which was still remaining. She also wondered how people asking for bhiksha were allowed inside the temple premises. A thought crossed her mind, "is this Baba?". However, she dismissed the idea thinking that it was her imagination. Next day was Vijayadashami - Baba's Mahasamadhi day. She felt that she should feed some poor person before leaving Shirdi without being surrounded by too much crowd. To her surprise, after she finished lunch she saw a poor boy asking the restaurant manager something to eat. Considering this as the best opportunity, she asked the hotel manager to pack some food for the boy and his family. At this very moment, a "Palki" procession was passing through the streets of the hotel. The participants of the procession were dressed like Baba and his devotees of yesteryears. She felt blessed that Baba fulfilled her heart's desire.

After returning to Bengaluru, she saw another message in the social media, "I came to you in Shirdi, but you didn't recognise me". Her eyes were bedewed with tears as she realised that the 'old man' who came to her asking for alms in the temple premises was Baba himself. She says even to this date, she gets goosebumps whenever she remembers this incident.

Felt guilty for not praying Baba

Lalitha of Bengaluru had to go to a local dispensary. Since she was in a hurry instead of her daily routine of lighting the lamp, decorating the shrine with flowers and praying to Baba etc, that day she left just after lighting the lamp.

As she came out of the house, she felt guilty that she did not have darshan of Sai Baba in her shrine. She therefore started looking for Baba's photo / idol / image in the vehicles that were passing by as usually most of the cars, autos, trucks, etc., carry Baba's images. But that day not a single vehicle had Baba's image. She says, "I could have tried to see in my cell phone, but that thought never occurred to me. I was frantically searching for a photo or an idol of Baba but that day I could not see any."

With a heavy heart she entered CGHS dispensary and stood in the queue for registration and obtained her token number, but all the while her mind was engaged in finding Baba's image.

In the dispensary, she was desperately looking for Baba's photo in each and every room. She even tried to peep into others' cellphones to see if they had Baba's image as the screensaver. However, she was not able to come to terms with the fact that she ignored Baba in a hurry and that she felt like having committed a grave mistake. She said, "This haunted me so much that I thought that I am not a true devotee of Baba and that's the reason Baba is not giving me His darshan".

While she was waiting for her turn, one of her friends came there with his 92 years old father. He was in the queue ahead of her and he entered the doctor's room. The doctor on seeing the details of the patient on the computer found out that it was the birthday of the patient. Greeting him on his birthday the doctor gifted him a small desk calendar.

Lalita said, "he came out smiling at me and said that his father received a gift of a desk calendar from the doctor on his birthday. Unlike my nature, suddenly I asked him to show me the calendar. I don't even know why I asked. He gave the calendar which had 12 different photos of Baba for 12 months. Seeing this beautiful form of Baba, tears started rolling down my eyes. I had asked for one darshan, but Baba has flooded me with 12 Darshans!!" she said with her eyes full of tears of joy. Her friend, knowing that she was a devotee of Baba, and looking at her emotions, asked her to keep the calendar.

"This was the most exciting moment in my life, never to be forgotten. The memory is still fresh in my mind and I got a reaffirmation on that day that Baba always longs for his devotees and would cross seven seas to fulfill the wishes of His devotees." Lalitha said happily.

Baba surprising with 'in person' Darshan to Mahtani

Natasha D Mahtani's father Doulat Shewak Mahtani was an ardent devotee of Baba. He started believing in Baba when he saw Baba's udi in his photo frame. He used to frequent Sai Centre in Penang, Malaysia, to find peace and divinity. One day when Natasha's father was driving in Batu Ferringhi, Malaysia, he saw Baba from his car. When he got down to see no one was there. The picture of Baba that Doulat Shewak Mahtani saw is given below.

From the year 1980 onwards till his attaining the Lotus Feet of Baba on January 4, 2021, he had been carrying in his wallet Baba's picture. When her father passed away Natasha kept his wallet in his shirt pocket. Nostalgically, Natasha says she often remembers and talks to her Dad and Baba as immediately after the passing away of her father, due to lockdown she felt very lonely and depressed.

Baba giving Darshan to his devotee

An anonymous devotee from Bengaluru says, "generally I recite Vishnu Sahasranama in my mind while driving to office. Around 2-3 months back, the moment I finished reciting Vishnu Sahasranama I asked Baba to bless me with His Darshan while still concentrating on driving. In one of the crosssroads, immediately after I crossed a traffic signal, I saw an elderly Muslim man looking and smiling at me. He was nodding his head up & down as if he was conveying something to me and also indicating with his right hand to proceed. I reached the office and submerged myself in my office work."

"In hindsight, I felt that it was actually Baba who appeared and confirmed to me that He is Baba because that's my regular route and I had never seen him before or after that day. It was then that I came to a firm conclusion that it was Baba; He fulfilled my wish. After this incident I could see a lot of positive energy in me" says the devotee.

"I never expected that, being a very ordinary person, Baba would fulfill my wish. In reality, Baba never distinguishes between any two devotees. To Him all are equal" says the devotee with a feeling of contentment and heart full of love for Baba.

Bow to Shri Sai
Peace be to all

Chapter 22

FOREWARNED

Anonymous devotee's regret

Anonymous devotee says that during the peak corona period her husband was transferred to another place - a hotspot for corona. As per her usual practice she cast lots in front of Baba asking His permission whether to go or not. She did cast lots thrice and every time, she got the answer as "NO". Devotee and all her family members told him not to go. But he was adamant and did not listen to anyone. It has always been her practice to abide by what the chit says. Since her husband was very adamant, unwillingly and half-heartedly she accompanied him to his place of posting.

Within a few weeks of reaching the new place her husband had breathlessness and had to be admitted to the hospital. Immediately, as per her practice she opened up a random page in Sri Sai Satcharitra which turned out to be chapter 31 and the story was about the passing away of Sanyasi Vijay Anand in the presence of Baba.

In the hospital, the hospital authorities admitted him in the corona ward even before a corona test. Next day his corona report turned out to be negative. Still the hospital authorities insisted that his symptoms are similar to corona and refused to shift him to the general ward. Seeing the corona negative report, the devotee was very happy and totally forgot about her earlier reading of chapter 31.

During this period devotee and her daughter also turned out to be COVID positive and were in home isolation. This made the devotee extremely depressed and in that tension she couldn't even pray to Baba.

Devotee's husbabd expired on the 4th day of his admission in the hospital. Devotee, as per her usual practice, after the death of her husband, cast lots to check with Baba if her husband was COVID positive or not. She cast lots three times and all the time Baba's answer was **NO**. Even today the devotee and all the family members believe that he did not pass away due to COVID but out of fear, because while he was in the COVID ward two patients next to him passed away and one of his best friends also succumbed to corona which her husbabd learnt through WhatsApp message.

Even today the devotee remorsefully says, if only I prayed to Baba and sent Udi to my husband while he was in the hospital, either directly or indirectly, he would have been alive today. Just as any patient passes away due to lack of medication or medical care, devotee says her husband passed away due to non-availability of udi in the hospital and absence of her prayers to Baba. With great difficulty the family has come to terms that it is fate that has played its part and that they couldn't win over fate.

Suparna forewarned

Suparna of Orissa, says that after completing MBA she got a job in Bhubaneswar and hence she was staying 40 kms away from home. Her parents were staying with her brother in Cuttack. Since 2017, she was regularly doing seva in a nearby Sai temple, like distributing prasad, sending people in a queue in a disciplined manner for darshan etc. In the month of March 2018, her parents visited her and they went to a nearby Baba temple and had a good Darshan of Baba. The same night at around 2 a.m. Baba appeared to her when she was fully awake and keeping His hand firmly on her head said that she will lose her father within 6 months. Baba further asked her to be strong and that He was always by her side.

On August 14, 2018, her father was admitted to the hospital due to sudden kidney failure and passed away on September 4, 2018. She said "as I was mentally prepared for this, I behaved like a strong daughter.". She still feels the pressure of Baba's hand on her head and says that I love Sai but Sai loves me more.

Prior indication

Jyothi of Chennai says that when her father was hospitalised, as per her usual practice, she randomly opened a page in the Sai Satcharitra which turned out to be chapter 31 dealing with certain devotees and a tiger attaining moksha (liberation). She was shocked. But as the day passed she forgot about the reading. She kept praying to Baba for her father's quick recovery.

Then on the third day of her father's hospitalisation when she randomly opened the book for reading she got chapter 27 in which Baba asks Shama to read Vishnu Sahasranama while assuring Shama that it will do him good. Immediately she started reciting "Shri Rama Rameti..." and completed three rounds of 108 chanting. After a while, the doctors confirmed the news of her father's passing away.

Jyothi says that though she got all indications to this effect, her mind was not willing to accept and she kept praying to Baba to cure her father quickly. However, surrendering to destiny she says Baba's words can never be untrue. It is we who breed false hopes, despite the clear divine indication.

Bow to Shri Sai
Peace be to all

CHAPTER 23

TEMPLE MIRACLES

There are many Saibaba temples in Coimbatore. I have chosen to write about the following two temples that I visited.

Sri Naga Sai Temple, Coimbatore

In the year 1939, Sh. H.H.B.V. Narasimha Swamji along with Shri A.V. K. Chari and Shri. C. Varadaraja Ayyah and his brother Shri. C.V. Rajan started the Sai movement in Coimbatore and the first institution of Sri Sai Baba in Tamilnadu (erstwhile Madras province) was established in Coimbatore. The Institution was named as Sri Sai Baba and was open to the public for darshan. Swamji entrusted the Centre to Sri. A.V. K. Chari. In the year 1942, late Shri C. Varadaraja Ayyah donated about one acre of land at Mettupalayam Road and a thatched shed was erected at the donated land to house the Sri Sai Baba Mission which was later named as Sri Sai Baba Madam. The Sai Baba Madam was the meeting ground of Sai Devotees in Coimbatore City at that time. Sai Bhajans were held regularly on Thursdays & Sundays.

Miracle at the temple and naming of the temple "Sri Naga Sai"

On the evening of Thursday January 7, 1943, while worshipping Baba, the following miracle happened.

A shining and lustrous Cobra (Naga) small in size but possessing an unusually big hood with divine marks of Tripundra, Shanka and Chakra appeared before Baba's picture when the Bhajan was going on in full swing to the accompaniment of drum cymbals etc., with all the lights on. The Naga stood there in a pose of worship fully entranced in Baba's music. Waving of lights, aratis etc had no effect on Cobra. People were astonished to see the wondrous sight of the Naga with the hood spread. There was no fear for the snake; and the crowd poured in thousands to the spacious land of the Bhajan Madam to witness this auspicious Naga that lingered in the same spot for 17 hours. Reverentially, Baba devotees began to shower baskets and baskets of flowers on the Naga. The Cobra was submerged in a mound of flowers and remained immobile.

On the second day, a photographer came to take a picture of the Naga. No one had the courage to go near the naga. The only course open to them was to pray. Seemingly, hearing the prayers of thousands of devotees, the Naga jumped out of the flower heaps and posed for the photograph. Then on the second day Naga went around Sri Sai Baba's picture and slowly went out into the open and disappeared into a bush where later on ant-hill (snake's natural habitat) appeared. The place where the Naga disappeared is held as a 'Holy Ground' by devotees and from that day onwards Shirdi Sai Baba in Coimbatore is worshipped as "Sri Naga Sai".

A brief description of the above story is mentioned in Shri Sai Satcharitra (Tamil version) at the end of Chapter 35.

Sacred Stick : Another speciality of this temple is that the stick that has been used by Sai Baba has been brought from Shirdi. The holy stick is being used to bless all devotees who visit the shrine.

Shirdi Sai Baba (Sri Naga Sai) Marble statue of the deity, is the only statue that was installed and consecrated on 26-02-1961 by Sri Sathya Sai Baba during his lifetime.

Today, Sri Naga Sai Trust consists of the Holy Shrine of Sai Baba, Sai Baba Vidyalayam Middle School, Sai Deep Kalyana Mandapam and free Homeopathy Clinic.

(Source : official website of the temple)

Theethipalayam Temple

History : Early November 1995, Sri Logidass Swamigal established an ashram for worship of Sri Saibaba; he performed poojas for nearly 30 years in an old Baba temple at Coimbatore town. In this small place, situated 10 kms away from Coimbatore, he performed regular poojas and special importance was given to Annadhanam.

Swamigal attained samadhi on 29.9.1999, and the divine power of his "soul" has enabled the temple trustees to complete his vision and further carry on with lots of social activities. A Meditation Hall was constructed and consecrated on 6.3.2003, followed by Kitchen & dinning Hall Complex, Parayana Hall, etc.

Miracles of the Temple

(I) Baba's idol cleared without any hitch

In the middle of the year 2002, while in the process of establishing the meditation hall, Mrs. Rema Vijayakumar ordered a Saibaba marble statue from Rajasthan. Before installation of the statue in the temple complex, they had sent the statue to Shirdi shrine for being sanctified at Baba's Samadhi Mandir. After this process the statue was transported to Coimbatore. At the Karnataka-Tamil Nadu check post, the officials demanded Rs. 36,000/- as 12% entry tax as it is a marble item. The trustees of the temple did not have the money to pay and Mrs. Rema Vijayakumar, a staunch devotee of Baba, kept crying continuously praying to Baba for the safe arrival of the statue without payment of any tax. After about an hour or so, Shri Pichaimani of Erode, Tamil Nadu, who was serving as CTO at the Karnataka Tamil Nadu border check post, heard a voice, "release Baba's statue unconditionally". Hearing this voice, Shri Pichaimani came out and instructed his officials to clear the statue without charging 12% tax. The temple trustees view the whole episode as nothing but the divine play of Baba to fortify further their devotion towards Him. Sharing this episode with me, Shri Vijayakumar said Baba skilfully arranged the circumstances to ensure smooth arrival of the statue to the temple.

(II). Sparrow taking refuge in Baba

On the World Sparrows Day on March 20, 2019, during Kakad Aarti in the morning a sparrow came and sat on Baba's statue. It seemed as if the sparrow was seeking refuge in Baba asking help to restore their free movement which has been restricted due to pollution and urbanisaion. This reminds me of Chapter XI of Sri Sai Satcharitra wherein Baba with his control over the elements quelled the storm as pleaded by birds, beasts and men. A picture of a sparrow taking refuge in Baba given below.

(II). Feet of Baba's Marble Statue turned

On October 31, 2018, during the night Arati for a few seconds, the feet of Baba's marble statue turned towards the southern direction. A picture of Baba statue's legs turned towards the southern direction may be seen in the following photograph.

(Source : Shri Vijayakumar, Trustee, Theethipalayam Sai Baba Temple)

My personal experience at the temple

At present Theethipalayam, Coimbatore, Saibaba temple is run by Sri Vengusapriya Saibaba Anandhashrama Trust. Located in a calm and peaceful place and surrounded by eye soothing greenery with utmost cleanliness, this temple and its environment provides a natural atmosphere for a devotee to have a complete union with Baba. The serene atmosphere yields a wonderful ambience for prayer and meditation.

Bow to Shri Sai
Peace be to all

Epilogue

As soon as the message of my writing a book on Sai miracles spread around, I started receiving miracles from my friends, family and their friends and families and strangers. People enthusiastically shared their experiences and while sharing they re-lived their happy moments and listening to their miracle and happy mood while narrating, I wondered why didn't I write before? But, everything happens at the right moment and not when I decide. With the blessings of Sai Baba of Shirdi, and seeking His help to make me write through Him, I began this book on the auspicious "Vijayadashami" - Baba's punyatithi.

In Tamil Nadu, where I hail from, Vijayadashami is regarded as Vidyarambham, meaning introducing a child to the world of knowledge and the process of learning. It is also called "*Mudhal Ezhuttu*" (first writing) as a child learns alphabets on this day, be it any language. In fact, for me it is my "*mudhal putthagam*" (first book) started on the auspicious Vijayadashami Day. To make this event memorable for me, Baba, through Arun B Ghodke, made me visit Shirdi and honoured me to carry Baba's Palki and participate in the Palki procession, which will be cherished by me for a lifetime.

While writing this book, one thing became very evident to me that it is not me who is writing this book. It is Baba who is holding my hands and writing this book, as I neither have the ability nor the knowledge to write. I had doubts, if I will ever be able to complete it. But Baba was always behind me to encourage me. In fact, the title of the Book, "Power of two letters - BABA" was also selected by Him. Six of my suggested titles were rejected by Him. It would, therefore, certainly not be wrong if I say it is Baba Who wrote this book and not me.

While listening, reading, writing, proofreading and editing these miracles I used to have goosebumps. Slowly and steadily, I was driven closer and closer to Baba. As I conclude this book, I would certainly implore Baba to keep holding my hands and not make me stop writing as the amount of happiness, joy, pleasure that I derived during this period cannot be measured. I am indebted to the devotees who shared their experiences with me as they have become an instrument to move a step forward on the spiritual path.

Bow to Shri Sai
Peace be to all

SAI BABA AARTI

Aarti Sai Baba. Saukhyadatara Jiva. Caranarajatali Dyava dasa visava, bhakta visava. Aarti....

Jaluniya ananga. Sasvarupi rahe danga Mumuksa janandavi. Nija dola Sriranga. Dola Sriranga. Aarti...

Jaya mani jaisa bhava. Tayataisa anubhava Davisi dayaghana, Aisi tuzi he mava, tuzi he mava. Aarti...

Tumace nama dhyata. Hare Sansruthivyatha Agadha Tava karani. Marga davisi anatha, davisi anatha. Aarti...

Kaliyuga Avatara, Saguna Brahma sachara Avatirna zalase Svami Datta Digambara, Datta Digambara. Aarti...

Athan Divasa Gurvari.Bhakta kariti vari.Prabhupada Pahavaya Bhava Bhayanivari, bhayanivari. Aarti..

Maza nijadravya theva, Thava carana-raja-seva Magane heci aata, Tumhan devadideva, devadideva. Aarti...

Ichita Dina chatak Nirmala toya nijasukh Pajaven Madhava Ya Sambhala apuli Bhaka Apuli bhaka. Aarti....

MEANING OF AARTI

We do Aarti to Sai Baba, the soul and the giver of happiness to all. Give refuge to the downtrodden devotees who are at your feet. We do Aarti to you Sai Baba.

Burn the desires. To the seekers of Self, teach them the way to get Moksha (state of pure bliss). With their own eyes, they see the Lord Vishnu (Sriranga). We do Aarti to you Sai Baba.

You grant suitable experiences to everybody in accordance with their faith and devotion. O, the merciful one, such is your way.O kind one. We do Aarti to you Sai Baba.

Meditation of your name removes the worldly sufferings. Your actions are unfathomable. Show the path to unfortunate ones. We do Aarti to you Sai Baba.

In this age of Kaliyug (The dark and troublesome age of present), you are the true incarnation of Brahama, that has taken form and descended on this earth. You are also Swami Datta Digambar (Three-headed deity who is considered as a combined incarnation of Brahma-Vishnu-Maheh). Datta Digambar.We do Aarti to you Sai Baba.

On Thursdays, every week, the devotees take a trip (to Shirdi), to have a glimpse of the Lord's feet and to avert their worldly fears. We do Aarti to you Sai Baba.

The only wealth I desire is to serve at thy feet. O Lord of Lords. We do Aarti to you Sai Baba.

Just as the chatak bird desires to drink pure raw water, so O Lord! And kindly give me your assurance (that I will receive such direct knowledge). We do Aarti...

9 789393 388742

Printed by Libri Plureos GmbH in Hamburg, Germany